ON THE PORCH

ON THE PORCH

CREATING YOUR PLACE TO WATCH THE WORLD GO BY

JAMES M. CRISP AND
SANDRA L. MAHONEY

The Taunton Press

Text © 2006 by James M. Crisp and Sandra L. Mahoney

Photographs © 2006 on pp. ii, 13, 16–18, 21, 23, 28, 33, 35, 43, 76–77, 90–99, 124, 130 (left & right), 136, 138 (left & right), 156–161, 166–169, 174, 192–199 ©Rob Karosis; pp. iii, 62, 126–127 ©Robert Perron; pp. vi, 52–55 ©Ken Gutmaker; pp. vii, 40, 66, 101, 107 (top), 112, 119, 140, 171, 179, 182 ©www.carolynbates.com; pp. vii (bottom), viii, 4–5, 8–9, 20, 22, 29, 34, 37, 42, 44, 64–65, 67, 105–106, 107 (bottom), 109–111, 115–116, 120 (right), 121–122, 125, 128, 129 (top & right), 133, 135, 139, 142, 144 (middle & bottom), 145–150, 153, 155, 178 (bottom), 181, 188, 191 ©Brian Vanden Brink, Photographer 2007; pp. 3, 14, 30, 82 (before), 137 Courtesy James M. Crisp; p. 6, ©Todd Caverly, Brian Vanden Brink Photos; pp. 7, 36, 46–51, 84–89, 151 ©Chipper Hatter; p. 11 ©James West Photography; pp. 12, 19, 32, 103–104, 108, 134, 144 (top), 152, 178 (top), 190 ©Phillip Gould; pp. 15, 27, 39 ©Douglas Keister; pp. 24-25, 118 ©Sandy Agrafiotis; pp. 31, 82 (after), 143 Graziella Pazzanese; p. 41 ©George Heinrich; pp. 56–61, 63 (top) Courtesy Library of Congress, Historic American Buildings Survey (HABS); p. 63 (bottom) ©Gary Coates; p. 70: Courtesy Miller Nicholson Architects; p. 72–73 Courtesy OBL Architects; p. 74 Photographer unknown, Courtesy John Phares; p. 75 (top) Photographer unknown; p. 75 (bottom) ©Kevin Marlow; p. 78 (before) Paul Blum, Courtesy SALA Architects; p. 78 (after) ©Christian Korab; p. 79: ©Don Wheeler; p. 83: Dee Blackburn, AIA, Courtesy Studio 1 Architects; pp. 100, 129 (bottom), 173–177 ©Anne Gummerson; pp. 113, 162–165 ©Randy O'Rourke; pp. 117, 154 ©Tre Dunham, Fine Focus Photography; p. 120 (left) ©April Tome, Grapic Solutions; p. 131 ©Barry Halkin, Halkin Photography; p. 141: ©Kevin Harris; p. 170 Courtesy Pizg & Thompson; p. 180 Courtesy Harrison Design; p. 183 ©Philip Clayton-Thompson; p. 184 (top & bottom) ©Jennifer Brown; p. 185 ©Lee Anne White; p. 186 ©Tim Street-Porter; pp. 187, 189 Michelle Gervais, ©The Taunton Press, Inc.

Illustrations © 2006 by The Taunton Press, Inc.

The Taunton Press
Inspiration for hands-on living®

The Taunton Press, Inc., 63 South Main Street, PO Box 5506, Newtown, CT 06470-5506
e-mail: tp@taunton.com

Editors: Maria LaPiana, Erica Sanders-Foege
Jacket/Cover design: Scott Santoro, Worksight
Interior Design: Alison Wilkes
Layout: Susan Fazekas
Illustrator: Martha Garstang Hill

LIBRARY OF CONGRESS CATALOGING-IN-PUBLICATION DATA:
Crisp, James M.
  On the porch : creating your place to watch the world go by / James M. Crisp and Sandra L. Mahoney.
     p. cm.
  Includes bibliographical references and index.
  ISBN-13: 978-1-56158-849-7 (alk. paper)
  ISBN-10: 1-56158-849-0 (alk. paper)
  1. Porches. 2. Porches–Decoration. 3. Architecture, Domestic. I. Mahoney, Sandra L. II. Title.

NA3070.C75 2007
721'.84–dc22

                                              2006029896

Printed in Singapore
10 9 8 7 6 5 4 3 2 1

The following manufacturers/names appearing in *On the Porch* are trademarks: Bear Board™, CorrectDeck®, Home Depot®, Target®, Thonet®, Trex®, UL®

Dedications

I would like to dedicate this book to my husband Robert, and my sons, Rob and Garrett, as well as to my mother and father, Carole and Francis Macek. Thank you for your patience and support. May we have many relaxing hours in our future for spending time together on a porch. — S.L.M.

To the owners of my two favorite porches: My mother Lucille Hill, whose porch often gives me shelter, and Bob and Pam Ferris, whose porch is a stage for their many grandchildren. To my wife Alicia and daughters Abigail and Shelby, to whom I dedicate both this book and my heart. — J.M.C.

Acknowledgments

The creation of a book is truly a collaborative effort, not unlike the process of designing and building a home. We have been very fortunate to work with a great group of people and we have many, many people to thank and acknowledge. First, thanks are due to executive editor Pam Hoenig for getting the ball rolling on this project by presenting her concepts of what a book on porches should include and for encouraging us along the way. We certainly want to thank the team at The Taunton Press, who contributed to the book and assisted two novice authors on the steep learning curve of book publication. We especially depended upon Wendy Mijal and Katie Benoit, who helped us with the plethora of photographs that are so integral to the book, and to Erica Sanders-Foege for her help in pulling the project together as deadlines approached. Most especially, we want to extend sincere appreciation and gratitude to Maria LaPiana, our editor, who translated our ideas into readable text and helped us find our voice. The project would have been much less without her yeoman efforts and able contributions.

This book is most especially a visual experience, and for that we depended on very capable and talented photographers, including Rob Karosis, who contributed so much to the book. We want to thank the homeowners, architects, and photographers who responded to our call for submissions. Special thanks go to the owners and designers of the portfolio projects. These homeowners were gracious and extraordinarily generous when they opened their homes for us to photograph their porches. Last but not least, thanks go to the photographers of the Historic American Buildings Survey.

We would also be remiss if we did not thank our coworkers at Crisp Architects for their assistance and patience. They were always there for us when we needed an extra hand and to pick up the slack when we were stretched thin.

Sandee would like to extend special thanks to Jimmy for affording her this opportunity. His trust, encouragement, and support have been most appreciated.

Finally, Jimmy would like to thank Sandee, without whose talent, organization, and hard work this book could not have been written.

Contents

Introduction

Across America, and certainly in our experience as architects in the Hudson River Valley, not far from New York City, there is a growing trend toward homes that are *livable*, homes that foster family ties and connections with nature. Homeowners everywhere are clamoring for comfort. Our clients consistently ask us to design homes that will allow them to take a breather from the breakneck pace of busy lives, to unwind, and to spend time with loved ones. And so, no matter how small or grand the project, we prescribe a porch; in our opinion, it's the perfect antidote to a hectic and harried lifestyle.

A while back we published an article on porches in Taunton's *Inspired House* magazine, and in so doing came to realize that porch design really was second nature to us: It's what we do. There are very few homes or additions that are designed at Crisp Architects that do not include some kind of porch. This book is a natural extension of our professional experience, as well as our personal lives.

In the house where Sandee grew up, the door between her screened porch and kitchen was thrown open in early May and was rarely closed again until late September. That porch was the hub of family life all summer long; it was where family members ate, talked, read, and entertained friends—there was even a hinged screen panel that swung open so they could pull in laundry from the clothesline without stepping outside.

Jimmy's affinity for a good old-fashioned porch comes from growing up in the South, where porch-sitting is part of the culture. Today, although he lives in the Northeast, his life continues to be enriched by porches: from the small covered entry at the back of his house to his in-laws' impossibly narrow porch that nevertheless becomes a comfortable gathering place for family the minute the weather warms up.

We were both delighted and impressed by the scope and quality of the porch projects we reviewed for inclusion in this book. We found that what we suspected was true: Porches are adaptable and dynamic. Homeowners and architects everywhere are interpreting them in unique ways to suit surroundings and pocketbooks, climate and terrain, tastes and lifestyles.

We open the book with an overview of the porches we found, and define six types—many of which overlap—so you can begin to form an idea of how you would most likely use a porch of your own. Next, we discuss the relationship between the porch and the house and share some transformations that are nothing short of extraordinary. Then we dissect the parts of every porch and suggest a wealth of possibilities to consider when designing your porch (or making improvements to the one you already have). Finally, we offer some ideas for enhancing your porch, including furnishings and greenery that add finishing touches.

We think it's easy to see why the porch has become an American icon—and we hope this book will provide you with the information and inspiration you need to create one of your very own. It's our pleasure to share with you the idyllic place we've come to know and love so well.

CHAPTER 1

The Porch You Choose

O ne of the abiding pleasures of a porch is that it can be useful and beautiful at the same time. Fundamentally, it offers shelter and extra living space, but a porch is much more than a place to plant a rocking chair. As you'll see in the pages that follow, a porch has the power to literally transform the look of your home.

Most porches are not designed to be all things to all people. If you like the look of a porch (and you probably do or you wouldn't be reading this) and you think there's a porch in your future, take a few minutes with this first chapter. Here we've identified six types of porches based on their primary purpose, because we believe if you want to add a porch to an existing house—or want to improve the porch you have—it's important to think about how you plan to use it. This is not to say a porch can have one purpose only, but it's a start. The finer points of porch design and building will come later.

This casual country porch offers shelter, atmosphere, and a peek-a-boo water view.

This type of porch makes a good first impression. It's usually at the front of the house, where proportion and details are best appreciated.

At our firm, we try to work porches into almost every project, and in the process we've found that they can be adapted to almost any architectural style—or lifestyle. To that end, the porch profiles that follow are meant as general guidelines, not strict schematics. You may find that the porch you pictured as pure architectural ornament invites pleasant visits from neighbors. Or you may discover that the far side of a grand porch designed for entertaining is an ideal sanctuary when company's coming. Porches inspire happy accidents like these.

As you begin to think about building a porch, take a close look at porches you find attractive (in books and magazines, and in your neighborhood) and try to determine what it is you like about them. At the same time, take note of porches you don't like; you can learn as much from a porch that doesn't work as you can from one you think is perfect

A Porch with Curb Appeal

Simply put, a porch with curb appeal is there for show; it exists to enhance the appearance of your home. But good looks are just the beginning; a well-designed porch can add character, balance, substance, and symmetry to a house, while helping to distinguish it from its neighbors.

This type of porch can truly make over a home's demeanor. A cozy portico can scale down an imposing, two-story house, making it appear less

Nestled into a nook and surrounded by flowering plants, a small sitting porch calls attention to an otherwise common colonial. There's no architectural fanfare; simple fluted columns define the space and link it to the house.

A small-scale but immensely charming portico defines the façade of a storybook cape. What it lacks in size the entry more than makes up in sweet colonial detailing; a hanging lantern and door hardware complete the perfect picture.

formal, whereas a porch with classical columns and a pediment can dress up a nondescript brick box. A gabled "farmhouse" porch can give a cookie-cutter colonial a warmer, more welcoming feel.

On a street where homes are of a similar style, or even exactly alike, porches can allow homeowners to express their individuality. Sandee recently toured a new community in North Carolina where porches have made a noticeable difference in the overall look and feel of the streetscape. Only five house plans were used throughout this development of some 150 homes, but because each house features its own porch design (from simple entry covers to wraparounds), the homes look distinctive and the community feels richly textured and diverse.

Details make the difference

Because a curb-appeal porch is often smaller in scale, you can get substantial visual impact for a relatively modest investment through the thoughtful use of some architectural elements: roofline, eaves, columns, railings, steps, post bases and caps, and decorative millwork.

It's important that your home and its porch be seen as a coherent whole, not separate structures that have been cobbled together. A porch should look like it has always been there. Here's how to do it:

• Design with scale and proportion in mind; scale is how the porch relates to the overall size of a house, whereas proportion is how it relates to other features, such as windows and doors (see "A Good Fit," p. 68).

• Use materials that are appropriate to the house and its surroundings. For example, there's nothing to say a brick home can't have a wood porch, but the porch should have some materials in common with the house, such as a brick floor or steps, or brick-clad post supports.

It's good form to repeat architectural details. A triangular window over a small, embellished porch has more impact when the shape is mirrored in the porch roof and detailed pediment.

Mixing and matching is perfectly acceptable when designing a curb-appeal porch. Scalloped shingles evoke a Victorian feel, which is reinforced by deeply turned posts and balusters. The robin's egg trim color connects the porch to the house, allowing the white balusters and brackets to stand out.

Color is fundamental to a well-designed porch, but less can be more. By keeping porch colors consistent with those on the house, even the simplest design details stand out, such as a metal shed roof with exposed eaves underneath.

- Repeat architectural details. If the main house has dentil moldings on the eaves, for example, this would be a nice detail to repeat, perhaps on a different scale, on the eaves of the porch.

- Keep colors consistent. Coordinate paint colors on your porch with those used on window or roof trim.

Not just another pretty space

If your house looks appreciably better because of the porch you added on, you could say it has done its job. But most porches (pretty ones included) can also serve as transition spaces or buffers, or even features that redirect traffic in and around your home—if your site and setback requirements will allow (see "Zoning, Setbacks, and Other Laws of the Land," on the facing page).

In many suburban settings where houses are close to one another and to the street, a narrow porch can function as a "screen" between public and private zones, easing the transition from one to the other. It can also serve to connect the house to the neighborhood by orienting the entrance to the street, making it comfortable for a visitor to approach.

A porch that is visible from the street (but not facing it) can also be used to direct visitors to an entrance other than the front door. A covered entry at the side of the house, perhaps alongside the driveway and/or garage, provides an informal invitation for friends and family to enter the house through the practical mudroom instead of the fussy foyer.

Another plus: Even a narrow porch offers at least some overhead protection from the elements. Be sure your porch roof extends at least 4 ft. from the house, and guests will appreciate coming in out of the rain while they wait to be invited in.

Zoning, Setbacks, and Other Laws of the Land

Before you get too involved in the design of your porch, you'll want to do some homework on your property. Whether you live in a densely populated city or on the outskirts of a cow town, there is a governing body that regulates how you can—and cannot—develop your building site.

You'll need to consider zoning regulations that may include the following:

• Minimum setbacks from your property line (front, back, and sides)

• Percentage of your property that can be covered with a structure

• Percentage of your property that can be covered with hardscape, such as terraces, walks, driveways, etc.

Your porch design may also be limited by building-height restrictions in your neighborhood. Although a porch is usually lower than the main house, there are cases (as in a porch with two or more stories), where the porch roof could end up being the highest point of the house.

It is the homeowner's responsibility to comply with a municipality's building regulations. Where to begin? Start by examining your deed to determine if there are any restrictions or covenants placed on your property. Next, run your plans by the local building and zoning depart-ment, which you'll be required to do anyway in order to obtain a building permit.

If you have your heart set on a design that doesn't comply with your town's zoning laws, you can usually request a variance. It has been our experience that if your neighbors are amenable to your plans (and there are no safety issues involved), you have a fighting chance of winning approval. Keep in mind that the variance application procedure can be complex and time consuming, so we often advise our clients to do an informal poll of their neighbors before they invest a great deal of time and energy.

Under special circumstances, a porch can actually be taller than the main house. That wouldn't typically pose a problem in a rural area or on a very large lot, but a variance might be necessary in a neighborhood with height restrictions.

This porch is an outdoor getaway, a retreat where you can escape the public areas of your house and yard.

The courtyard is the thing that makes a ground-level, open-brick porch feel private. Its boundaries are defined by its distance from the arched opening to the courtyard, oversize columns, and a change in flooring.

The Privacy Porch

Porches are great gathering places, but one of the things we love best about them is that they can be very private, too. Where else can you daydream, read, nap, sit quietly with a baby in your arms, or chat in hushed tones with a loved one—all while enjoying a breath of fresh air?

There are three kinds of privacy porches: The first is truly inaccessible and/or not visible by anyone but the users; the second offers seclusion at least some of the time, depending on the hour, the season, or even the weather; and the third, although technically in full view, feels protected and removed because of its surroundings.

Picture a tiny recess in the third-story gable of a Queen Anne–style home and you've got the first kind: a private porch you can't get to from the ground. In period homes, these porches were sometimes placed at the top of a winding set of narrow stairs. We added this kind of porch to a home we designed, recessing it between gabled wings on the second story. The only way onto it is through a door in the master bedroom. Although they can see for miles into the valley surrounding their home, the homeowners are completely hidden from view when they sit outside.

The second or "occasional" private porch is one that Jimmy knows well. When he visits family in rural Louisiana he stays in a modest guest house with a porch overlooking a lazy river. He makes a point of getting up early just so he can sit out there alone, listen to the wildlife, and watch the river

Accessible only from the master bedroom suite, this private, second-story porch affords a spectacular view of meadows, fields, and farms beyond the homeowners' property.

13

You can't get there from here. A sheltered recess hidden away in the third-story gable of a busy Victorian provides shade, privacy, and a clandestine place from which to survey the yard and gardens below.

flow by. It's even better, he says, when a gentle rain taps on the tin roof and breaks the surface of the river into tiny wavelets. But it's not always so peaceful. Because the porch is visible from the courtyard between the houses, its privacy depends on the time of day and, sometimes, the weather. If there is family activity in the yard, Jimmy's private perch quickly becomes a community porch, but first thing in the morning he may as well be on a mountaintop.

In contrast, Jimmy remembers hiding in plain sight on the third kind of porch, a tiny one off the second story of a house he lived in as a child. Overlooking a busy boulevard in Galveston, Texas, Jimmy spent hours on this porch, gazing past traffic to the Gulf of Mexico. He'd peer through a small telescope at cargo ships, freighters, and shrimp boats, watching storms come in off the Gulf. Far from the bustle of the boulevard below, Jimmy always felt protected, and passersby rarely seemed to notice him.

Make a private spot even more so

Whichever privacy porch you prefer, location is your most important consideration. Privacy from the outside world can be accomplished simply by locating the porch away from neighbors and traffic, whereas privacy within the home may be more difficult to manage. Think about how you'll get to your porch; one way to keep intrusions to a minimum is to limit access to a tucked-away bedroom or the end of a long hall.

A secluded site provides a natural barrier to the outside world, but most homeowners have neighbors, so a truly private porch may be hard to come by. Remember, even if you add onto the side of the house that no one can see now, that can change if someone builds on land next door.

A porch that's private in the early morning may become less so as the day wears on. It's certainly true of the porch on a guest house Jimmy frequents when visiting family in Louisiana. He likes being the first one up and out so he can enjoy the quiet morning.

Sleeping Alfresco

Because the Victorians believed that sleeping in the open air was healthy, they added sleeping porches to many of their homes. The sleeping porch was often a screened, second-story gallery that was used by the infirm—as well as by overflow guests.

When air conditioning came along, scores of sleeping porches were enclosed, and this charming, evocative feature all but disappeared from America's architectural landscape.

The Philip Hart House in Millbrook, N.Y. is a stunning center-hall Federal home built in 1800. Historic records show that in 1889 the Hart family added a two-level porch to their home. The second-floor porch was screened in and used by the Harts' daughter-in-law, who suffered from tuberculosis.

Nearly a century passed, and the home was purchased by David and Nan Greenwood, whose restoration included replacing the porch decking and screens so they could use the space.

Today, the Greenwoods refer to the sleeping porch as their "summer room," where they and their guests go to catch a breeze and get a bird's-eye view of the grounds below.

And yes, on hot summer nights they sleep there, too.

Usually connected to a second-floor hallway, sleeping porches may be located at the front or the back of a house. The area below the Greenwoods' porch also serves as the covered rear entry into the home's center hall.

Added years after the house was built, the sleeping porch was faithfully restored. The floor was covered with painted canvas, a traditional water-proofing measure.

Think creatively. You may live on Main Street, but if your porch is 20 ft. above the sidewalk no one will know you are there. If your only choice is a porch that sits closer to the ground, then look into ways you can artfully shelter your porch from view.

When picking your location, take note of any natural screening already provided by existing trees and shrubs. If that's not an option, you can create that screening yourself through strategic plantings (see Chapter 4). Be sure to check with a landscape designer or your local nursery to determine which varieties will grow well (and quickly) in your area. Remember that sun and shade are important considerations, and if you live where there is an abundant deer population, it makes sense to choose plants that don't appeal to deer. Finally, keep in mind when budgeting that the larger the plant, the greater the cost.

Blinds and shutters are a good way to create privacy, even if your next-door neighbor is only a few yards away. You can install exterior-grade shutters (fixed or hinged, with operable or fixed louvers) or blinds (that stack or roll up) in many standard sizes, or you can have them custom-made to fit almost any opening. Sure, you can see through some blinds and screens if you really try, but they do create a visual barrier. Lattice can work in the same way to shield your porch from view. Don't forget that blocked views also mean blocked light, so use blinds and shutters sparingly unless you want to cut down on heat gain or glare as well.

Blinds and shutters can keep out prying eyes even while filtering sunlight. Fixed louvers can be installed top to bottom at either end of a porch, or they can be fitted to fill the space between the railing and the roof.

Nature can make any porch a private one. Strategically planted trees and shrubs can screen a porch as well as any remote piece of property, with a bonus: Broad leafy plants do much to shade and cool a porch, too.

This is a porch that invites gathering. Family and friends should be able to sit, stand around, and move through the space with ease.

Lush tropical trees and a refreshing in-ground pool invite entertaining in grand style nearly all year long. A backyard of generous proportions demands a porch that is appropriately spacious and open, with high ceilings and towering pillars that define areas for sitting, socializing, and poolside lounging.

The Entertaining Porch

Growing up in the South, Jimmy's idea of the quintessential entertaining porch is a graciously appointed grand veranda filled with well-dressed guests sipping mint juleps.

At the same time, he knows you don't need a mansion or miles of balustrade to have a very social porch. Every morning on the way to work he passes the home of family friends, a small farmhouse built in the 1800s. The modest back porch on that house has seen more wedding showers, graduation parties, and other festivities than anyone can count. Why? Overlooking the yard where children often play, the porch is a good size, at some 9 ft. by 30 ft. It's spacious enough to allow room for a table and several flexible seating arrangements. And because there are doors to both the living room and dining room, it invites a circular traffic pattern in and out of the house.

There are porches to suit every entertaining style, and to make sure yours ends up being a perfect fit you need to honestly assess the kind of entertaining you'll want to be able to do, as it will affect the location of your porch and how big it should be. If your house is a magnet for kids, friends, and relatives and you never know how many you'll be having for dinner,

Summer parties and holiday picnics are easily imagined on a classic country porch, replete with wicker chairs, table, and settees. Hanging plants and bunting give the space an especially festive feeling.

Truly formal affairs are few and far between, so a cozy space filled with casual furniture is an ideal multiuse entertaining porch almost all the time. Artfully arranged tables and chairs promote dining, conversation, and kicking back.

you'll want a porch that can hold them all—preferably off the kitchen and steps from the backyard. If, however, you tend toward more intimate or formal gatherings, you might prefer a small porch you can access only through French doors in the dining room.

Design a porch that does it all

The best entertaining porch is designed for multiple activities—but it doesn't have to be huge. By simply defining discrete areas for conversation and dining, you can create the illusion that your porch is larger than it really is.

Of course, if your site will allow, a wraparound porch does it all. It can provide plenty of room for dining on one side and mingling on another. You can gain even more space by bumping out a corner to create a spacious area dedicated to eating out. If you really want to spread out, you can open up a corner and link the porch to a freestanding gazebo by laying down a narrow walkway between the two.

Next, think about your surroundings. Although an entertaining porch need not be as secluded as a privacy porch, you probably don't want to hold dinner parties in full view of your neighbors. For this reason, you'll want to locate your porch away from your street and property line, and possibly build in some privacy with fencing or hedges.

Linked to the main house by a pathway open on both sides, a freestanding porch provides a completely separate space for entertaining. Another door on the far side of the porch invites a circular traffic pattern back to the house, the food, and the drinks.

Dining out—in style

Whether you prefer to cook, cater, or call for takeout, food and drink are mainstays of an entertaining porch. If you think you'll serve frequent meals on yours, be sure you have ready access to the kitchen. A good way to cut down on trips to and from the kitchen is to add a pass-through window directly onto the porch. Place it over a kitchen countertop and you'll get a welcome source of light in the bargain.

If you like to grill, you'll want your porch near the barbecue. Or better: Build a grill directly into the porch itself. We've designed several that back up to indoor fireplaces (the grill and fireplace have separate flues, but share the masonry of the chimney). You could even go all out and outfit your porch with a pizza or bake oven. Remember, though, that outdoor cooking areas pose potential fire hazards, and their construction is restricted by your municipality's building codes. Built-in barbecues should be equipped with hoods to contain upward-reaching flames, and it's essential that your contractor follow all installation requirements as spelled out by the manufacturers of grills and wood-burning ovens.

Locating a wet bar on your porch can cut down on trips to the kitchen, and it's handy for cleanup, too. But if you live where temperatures drop below freezing, you must be able to shut off water lines, drain pipes, and add antifreeze to the drains in winter, so be sure to consult a plumber.

Some counter space is a good idea for serving buffet style, and if you build in a few electrical outlets you can run the blender or brew fresh coffee, too (see "Bringing Power to Your Porch," p. 151).

The serious cook won't miss a minute of the porch party if the grill is within reach. Add a cooktop and pizza oven, all built directly into a stone wall, for all the comforts of a well-equipped kitchen.

How Much Room Do You Really Need?

Homeowners often make the mistake of allowing just enough space on the porch for furniture, without thinking about how they'll move around it. Although it's possible to squeeze quite a few chairs around a table, your guests will be much more comfortable if they can pull them out, stand behind them, and allow others to get by. You've also got to allow room for some table "push back." As guests relax, their impulse is to push away from the table, and you don't want them wedged up against a wall.

Use these minimum clearances as a guide:
1. To accommodate a small café table with two chairs against the wall (and room to walk past), a 6-ft.-deep porch will suffice.

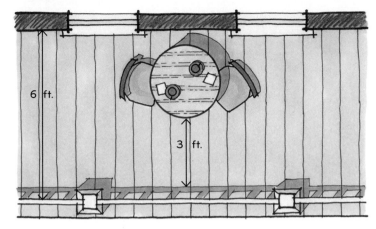

BISTRO TABLE

2. A dining table requires at least 3 ft. at each end and 3 ft. at both sides to allow room to pass. For example, for a 4-ft. by 9-ft. table your minimum porch size should be 10 ft. deep by 15 ft. long.

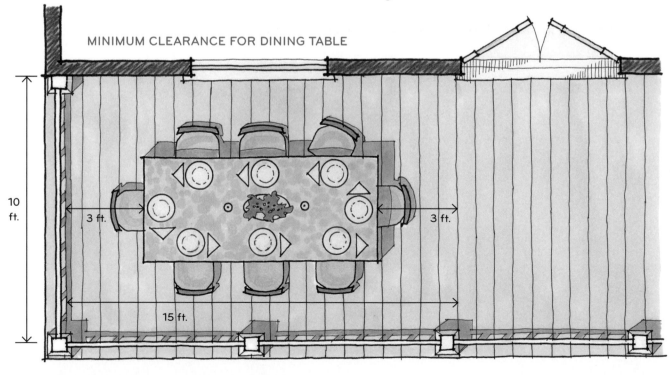

MINIMUM CLEARANCE FOR DINING TABLE

Add creature comforts for easy living

If you like the idea of easy, casual entertaining on your porch, bring a bit of the indoors out. For starters, your guests will appreciate a little climate control, especially if the temperatures where you live tend toward extremes.

You can build radiant heating into the decking to warm guests in chilly weather (and to keep ice and snow at bay in winter). A natural-gas heater can be installed along with your gas grill or you can choose a portable patio heater that uses bottled fuel—kerosene, butane, or propane—and can warm an area 20 ft. around.

For a guaranteed summer breeze, a ceiling fan is the classic choice. With the many sizes and styles available today, you can select a fan that both cools the space and complements your porch architecture.

Lighting can play an important role in creating ambience on your entertaining porch. You have a multitude of choices—from wall sconces to electric (outdoor-rated) or candlelit chandeliers. Recessed lights work well and are easy to dim to suit the mood. Task lighting makes cooking and mixing drinks easier, and if your porch is large or has separate seating arrangements it is a good idea to specify independent lighting controls.

And don't forget the music. Outdoor speakers are easy to install and you can use touch pads to control selection and volume.

As you begin to design the perfect porch in your mind, you'll want to refer to Chapter 4, "The Finishing Touches," where we'll discuss creature comforts in greater detail.

A cooling breeze from a ceiling fan can make all the difference when company comes. Broad blades and complementary colors add style as well as comfort.

The vista is the thing. This porch offers both refuge and outlook, whether your view is of the ocean or of a flower garden.

An already spectacular view is enhanced when a porch is elevated even a few steps off the ground. The post-and-rail system was kept simple to keep fussy details from obstructing the long vista of fields, mountains, and sky.

The View Porch

Of course, every porch has a view of one kind or another. But the best view porch is one that overlooks something pleasing or evocative.

One of the homes we designed opens onto a breathtaking vista of the Hudson Valley and beyond to the Catskill Mountains. The owners bought the property for its extraordinary views and there was never a question that the home they built would have to take full advantage of them. The result was a porch that wraps around three sides of the house.

Granted, not everyone has the luxury of a jaw-dropping view, but you don't need acres of land to like what you see. Jimmy lives in an 18th-century farmhouse that was added onto over time, and his porch is as modest as they come. And yet, the shallow, covered-entry porch at the back of the house has become his very own, tiny reviewing stand. Looking onto an enclosed yard with a stone patio and dogwood tree, Jimmy's favorite view is of his young daughters tossing a ball around with their two Chesapeake Bay retrievers on lazy summer afternoons.

If you're lucky enough to have a porch with an especially long vista, you enjoy a unique kind of entertainment, because there's nothing quite like watching a summer storm roll in while sitting protected on a cozy porch. From miles away you can see the sky change color, until the clouds arrive overhead and the first raindrops fall.

A water view enhances the intrinsic value of any porch. A rocker perched on the cool corner of a summer cottage is the perfect spot to catch a breeze over an inlet and watch boats go by.

Porches that project out over a sloped lot maximize views in every direction. Extensive support is needed, however; native lumber elevates a series of porches and decks on the low side of the site.

Any view that overlooks a body of water is one that can change dramatically. From a shift in wind direction, to the swooping of seagulls on the water's surface, to the sudden appearance of a sailboat, water views can be both dynamic and mesmerizing.

A good view can present a challenge

If you have a spectacular vantage point, there's a good chance you have some worries, too. When your view is a beauty, the conditions surrounding it can be beastly.

A case in point is a porch that overlooks the ocean. Porch materials that are exposed to unbroken sunlight, rain, and salt will deteriorate much faster than those used in shady, inland neighborhoods. Homeowners with ocean views should choose the most durable porch materials they can afford, as well as paints and sealers designed for the rigors of a coastal climate.

Wind is another concern. Although no porch can withstand the worst hurricane-force winds, you can take measures to limit damage from lesser storms. Roof rafters should be firmly connected to posts, beams, and the walls of the home, and posts should be anchored securely to foundations or piers. Keep in mind that on some hills and mountains the wind is much stronger than it is in nearby valleys.

A view porch on a sloped site can present another kind of structural challenge. If your house sits at the top of the slope you'll probably need to level the area under and around the porch with large amounts of earthen fill. If you want your porch to project out over the slope you'll need to support it with posts and beams or a foundation wall. In some areas of the

The simplest garden structure is the center of attention when framed by tall posts and a rhythmic balustrade. It can be as practical as a garden shed or as fanciful as a pigeonnier.

country it's not uncommon to hit rock while excavating, which can require poured footings (concrete pads that rest on rock or solid soil) or structural posts attached firmly to solid rock. In others areas, mudslides are a serious concern and porches in those regions should be very thoughtfully engineered.

Remember that all porches should be designed for your specific site by an architect or engineer who is familiar with the code requirements in your town as well as the characteristics of your region (from earthquakes and mudslides to high winds and soil erosion).

Not much to look at? Not to worry

Having a porch with a view may seem a little like being tall: You either are or you're not. Well, that's not necessarily true. It is possible to create a view where there was none before; it can be anything from a flower garden to a beautiful tree surrounded by open space.

Louisiana architect A. Hayes Town was a master at creating special views around the homes he designed, mostly in the South. He designed Zen-like views with brick arches and hedges and delighted in placing small structures in the open landscape. By framing it with plastered brick columns, Town created a complex and multilayered view from the porch on his own home: You look out across a stone patio punctuated by sculptures and specimen trees, through an arch in the brick wall, to a garden structure surrounded by even more beautiful landscaping.

In the flatlands of Louisiana, if you want a view other than flora, fauna, or the horizon, you have to create it. A classic example is a charming *pigeonnier*—a model of traditional form and attention to detail—that was designed by Town specifically to be viewed from a porch.

Close-in scenes can complement distant vistas. The view from a well-sited porch can change seasonally if a garden is planted nearby.

This friendly porch connects to the street. It's designed to invite conversation and a sense of community.

A neighborly porch is one that sits close to the house next door, but more than that, it's a porch furnished in an inviting way. Bright red rockers, soft chenille pillows, and seasonal greenery send greetings to the street.

The Neighborly Porch

It's retro-chic and advocates of bringing back Main Street, U. S. A. are clamoring for its return. Indeed, the neighborly porch may be the most iconic porch of all.

This porch is highly visible and always situated streetside, to allow you to see and be seen. It's both accessible and inviting, so porch-sitters can call out a greeting or exchange pleasantries within easy earshot of passersby.

But there's more to a neighborly porch than its proximity to the sidewalk. This type of porch needs to be an open structure, not one sheltered from view with heavy lattice or shrubs. It has low railings and broad, wide steps that encourage sitting for a spell. It can accommodate a chair or two (at least) and it wears homey touches—like hanging plants and pillows—very well.

Because the orientation of this porch is so focused on the street, it need not be very deep. Still, when space permits we like to use 9 ft. as a rule of thumb to allow for a rocking chair, plenty of leg room, and room to pass in front. But it's a guideline only. We have a friend whose porch is a scant 4 ft. deep and she says that's plenty for sitting and sipping wine with friends. She admits it can be a little tight; if you want to stretch your legs, you have to prop them up on the railing. Nevertheless, it's the most neighborly porch she's ever known. (She is thinking, however, that a nice improvement might be an extra wide handrail that could accommodate a glass or two).

An open structure and ample seating on a neighborly porch invite passersby and folks next door to stop a while and catch up.

Comfort and hospitality are key

Although every neighborly porch is designed primarily for sitting and visiting, it's important to consider when you are most likely to use it.

Our hard-working friend with the narrow porch seldom uses it in the daytime, so the sun is not a problem for her. But if you had a porch with a similar orientation and intended to use it primarily in the mid- to late afternoon, you'd want a means of controlling the sun to keep heat and glare in check. Your shading options include retractable blinds or canvas shades attached to beams in the ceiling. Both can easily be rolled up or moved out of the way as the sun moves on. Carefully placed trellises with climbing plants will do the trick, too, but be careful to leave plenty of space between and around the plantings or your neighbors won't be able to see in and your porch will lose its inviting feel.

The most neighborly porches we know have wide stairs, risers that aren't too steep, and treads deep enough to sit on—alongside a few clay pots brimming with seasonal plantings.

A formal home can still feel friendly with the right porch attached. Highly visible and accessible because of its low railing and proximity to the sidewalk, even this tall and proper structure allows passersby to see in and say hello.

Front and center, nothing says "Come on up" better than stairs that open to embrace visitors and direct them to the front door. What makes stairs welcoming? Shallow risers, deep treads, and smooth handrails that are easy to reach.

Good Porches Make Good Neighbors

The social nature of the porch resonates even with those who have no time to sit and pass some time. Many simply like the idea of sitting in wicker chairs, sharing stories and cool drinks.

We've seen renewed interest in the "neighborly porch" as the sign of an attitude shift, a yearning for community. This is evident in communities such as Seaside, Fla., which requires every home to have a front porch that is open to the street, and Laguna West, a pedestrian development near Sacramento, Calif., where porches (not garages) define the façades of houses.

We think that neighborly porches are gaining in popularity because they connect us in an increasingly disconnected world. Says architect Elizabeth Plater-Zyberk, "On the porch it's possible to participate in a public sense—and the public can participate in a homeowner's private world." The neighborly porch impacts us both locally and globally. It speaks of taking time for friends—as well as participating in the community of your block, your neighborhood, and your town or village as a whole.

"Porches are places for observing the world, for meeting for shelling peas, for courting, and for half a hundred

A simple and classic-looking porch with two ways to reach it captures the essence of neighborliness. Low-lying shrubs, distinct walkways, and a pair of screen doors into the house itself suggest that guests are welcome.

friends, for talking, for knitting,
other activities." — *Kenneth T. Jackson, in Crabgrass Frontier*

A porch as a room: This is an extension of your interior space that can be enjoyed in all but the worst weather.

The best place to locate a screened porch is near the rooms you already use most. By connecting a porch to a comfortable living room, both spaces enjoy a sense of roominess and views both in and out of the house are improved. A plus: A wall that opens, accordion-like, between the porch and the house.

The Screened Porch

We like to think of the screened porch as a way to have your cake and eat it, too. With a screened porch, you can enjoy gentle breezes, pleasant views, and fragrances from your garden, all while keeping insects at bay. It's no wonder it has become a mainstay of porch construction.

The screened porch, with its sense of enclosure, is the most roomlike of porches. It's where you can dine, play cards and board games with the family, write a letter, take a nap, or savor a summer novel—in essence, do all the things you can do indoors—but with no pesky mosquitoes or flies to bother you.

A screened porch can be a simple structure made of aluminum and screening materials set on an existing patio, or it can be an elaborate edifice of columns and timbers that, if designed well, will allow for year-round use.

Location, location, location

Because a screened porch can accommodate so much living, it should be connected to the house where you're most likely to use it. When a screened porch is attached to a family room or great room, both spaces benefit from shared vistas through open doors and an expanded sense of space. Locating a screened porch close to the kitchen allows for the easy transport of meals to the porch table.

Ideally, a screened porch should have dedicated spaces for conversation and dining and maybe a secluded corner for reading. We've found that too

An integrated screened porch shouldn't look like an add-on or feel like an afterthought. A well-designed space serves as a true indoor/outdoor room, as useful as it is visually appealing.

Screening can give, so it's important to build in a strong post-and-rail support system. A detailed balustrade designed to suit a rustic porch can dress up a porch's exterior even while protecting it.

often screened porches are simply not large enough, so give careful consideration to your furnishings: the size of your table and the number of chairs you plan to use on your porch, as well as the necessary clearance around them (see "How Much Room Do You Really Need?," p. 26).

Screens play a supporting role

The look of your porch depends in part on the screening you choose. Screening can run unobstructed from floor to ceiling, it can be divided by a rail 3 ft. or so from the floor, or it can rest on top of a kneewall.

We've found that a break in the span of the screen keeps the size of the screen panels manageable and allows for easy removal for storage and/or repair. A maximum size of approximately 4 ft. by 6 ft. works well, because most screening material can span this size and still remain taut.

All screening can give under enough pressure, so you may want more support to protect against falls, especially if your porch floor is higher than 30 in. off the ground. A railing system can provide that extra support, and if you install the rails on the inside your porch will look better from the outside, too.

Keep in mind that lower sections of screening are easily damaged (by furniture legs, kids, pets, and the inadvertent kick), so we often specify a decorative wood grid for protection and stability. Another option is to use a more durable product under the kneewall, such as lattice backed with screening or clear Plexiglas® sheets, which will preserve the view.

Experience has taught us that the screened porch ends up becoming such an integral part of a home's living space that many homeowners decide they want to use it for three seasons—and sometimes four. Even if you don't think you'll ever want to switch out your screens for windows, we advise that you engineer your porch for that possibility, as retrofitting can

A substantial screened porch added to the end of a house has the advantage of three wide-open sides. If windows will replace screens in colder weather, the structure must be engineered to support extra weight. This provides an opportunity to create a balcony above that is accessible from a second-story bedroom or hallway.

A pair of porches—one screened and one open—should share some design features. The same railing runs around both, and the openings framed between posts outside are repeated in the shape of screened panels.

be difficult and costly. Hind loads greatly increase with the installation of glass panels, so windows may not be an option unless your porch is designed to support them.

Many of the screened porches we've designed are open to the landscape on three sides, which maximizes the "fresh air" quality of the space. This makes it possible to design a flat roof over the porch and, with it, a second-story porch or an open deck accessible from an upstairs room. Because this option obviously adds new and greater bearing loads to your porch structure, make sure your engineer is aware of how you plan to use your upper levels. This is definitely something to think about if you are building new.

A screened porch can also be a hybrid of sorts. One part may be screened in (often a dining area), while the rest is left open. Because they're attached structurally, you'll want to keep them looking visually connected. If the open-air porch has a handrail on it, then continue that band at the same height on the screened section.

Although screening can keep out bugs, you may still need protection from the sun. Shutters, matchstick blinds, trellis panels, or roll-down canvas shades can all be integrated into your screened porch design.

There's no question that a screened porch allows a home to live larger. Its indoor/outdoor personality will make it a popular destination in all but the very worst weather conditions.

Screen Test

There are a variety of different screening materials to choose from. Find out which one is right for your porch.

	PROS	CONS
FIBERGLASS MESH	• Long lasting; easy to work with; won't discolor; available in gray, black, or charcoal and different mesh sizes; most inexpensive option	• Has a tendency to stretch and buckle when on the frame; tears easily
ALUMINUM WIRE MESH	• Tougher than fiberglass; resists stretching and tearing; resists corrosion	• Discolors over time
COPPER WIRE MESH	• Tougher than fiberglass or aluminum; holds its shape; ages to a natural patina	• No color option except brown; higher cost than aluminum or fiberglass
BRONZE WIRE MESH	• Stronger than copper; corrosion resistant; good in salt air; attractive natural color	• Expensive; not all mesh sizes are readily available
STAINLESS STEEL	• Very corrosion resistant and strong; nice silver gray color	• Very expensive

Southern Comfort

BEFORE

This modest street-side façade doesn't begin to suggest the grand entertaining porches that await guests out back.

John and Valerie Bergeron's home is a gracious and busy

Natchez,
Mississippi

place all year long, but it takes on special importance in the spring and fall, when the B&B known as Pleasant Hill is jam-packed with guests.

Years ago, when the couple bought the historic home in Natchez, Miss., they knew they'd need more room to accommodate overflow guests, but the rear of the house was boxed in, rather plain, and fairly useless. John consulted the Historic Natchez Foundation and discovered that a back porch had indeed existed at one time, but it had been more than mangled over the years. It seems that early on both ends of the porch were closed in, creating only a small open area in the middle. At some point that was closed in, too, so by the time the Bergerons came along there was no porch left.

It feels like a living room: The second-floor gallery is arranged with formal furnishings into a series of conversation areas, some that inspire socializing, like this one, and others that are more private.

Symmetry rules at the rear of the house, which is all about the loggia and the gallery. From a distance, it's hard to imagine the house without its statement porches—but they were not always there.

The simple detailing of painted wood balustrades on the gallery above softens the overall appearance of the porch.

Covered and Uncovered Space

They learned that an authentic, two-story, full porch would have had masonry piers on the first level, with posts and an open railing above. They set out to reconstruct that type of porch, but took license with some materials.

For example, they used antique brick for the piers and pressure-treated wood instead of traditional cypress. What's perhaps most interesting is that they left the upper level, or gallery, partially open to the sky. A mix of covered and uncovered space gave them flexibility and simplified the structural requirements necessary to extend the roof. This raised gallery offers flood protection and provides a place where guests can enjoy the sun and catch a breeze. Ceiling fans cool the part of the gallery that sits under the roof.

The ground below was excavated to allow a loggia to be built. Sheltered by the brick pillars, the loggia has a tinted concrete floor and is covered by

Softened by a dappled stain, the concrete floor is scored to keep the slab from looking monolithic. The color complements the red brick used for the piers.

Rhythm abounds on the upper porch. Fans are evenly spaced between exposed rafters on the ceiling, large windows flank the French doors, and rockers are lined up, ready for relaxation.

It's possible to enjoy the sun while sitting under cover on the cool loggia. Brick pillars frame a quiet contemplative view out to the garden.

a roof with exposed painted rafters. French doors connect the loggia to a garden room, which extends across the lower west side of the house. The lower level also includes four suites and a bar area accessible to the outdoors.

Because the Mississippi sun heats up so much in summer, the homeowners call the upper gallery the "morning porch," whereas the shaded loggia, which is quite a bit cooler later in the day, is the "afternoon or evening porch."

Plantation Living

The large addition has a decidedly plantation feel. Both porch spaces are furnished like living rooms, with plenty of comfortable rocking chairs, benches, and tables. Potted and hanging plants, fabric tablecloths, and soft cushions further enhance the indoor/outdoor feeling.

On both levels, the Bergerons sought to create views from the house through the new porches and beyond. Everything they decided—from porch furnishings to landscape design—was planned with that in mind.

A classic porch swing is made more comfortable with a soft seat cushion piled with accent pillows covered with indoor/outdoor fabrics.

The gallery beckons guests who enter from the entrance hall. Floorboards and rafters draw the eye out, increasing the perspective, which makes the porch seem deeper than it really is.

Seeing Double

This home was described as the "ugly duckling" of its

Palo Alto,
California

neighborhood in upscale Palo Alto, Calif. It was a misfit at best, with no relation in scale or style to the other homes on the street. For example, it was the only one-story structure. With a flat, nondescript façade and an undefined sense of entry, the house had no curb appeal at all.

The original house was actually two structures connected with a shed roof, and though it underwent a relatively substantial whole-house renovation, it is the porches—uniquely side by side as seen from the street—that set the tone for the home.

There were challenges. The house is situated in an established neighborhood of homes that are 50 years old (and older). As such, there were strict architectural review standards that had to be met. The resulting design is an interpretation of the Craftsman style evident in the area. The architect's mandate was to enhance the outdoor living spaces, to create a welcoming and sheltered entry, and to respect the street and neighbors.

From the street, the formerly unremarkable bungalow now presents a sweet Craftsman-style façade to passersby.

Exposed rafters and trim details evoke a Craftsman feel, but the architect was careful to create a pergola-like design and specify white trim to avoid making the small porch feel too heavy.

Inside the entry porch looking out, the stucco kneewalls provide enclosure, whereas the openness of the trim detail connects the space to the street.

The new façade and its porches were constructed of durable, low-maintenance materials like stucco walls, brick steps, concrete floors, and wood trim that are characteristic of California Craftsman-style architecture.

Side by Side

The dual porch spaces serve distinct purposes. A front sitting porch is at once neighborly and semiprivate, thanks to plantings that frame the street-side opening and the fact that you can only access this porch from the living room. Although there's no way for the neighbors to actually join you, it's a good place to greet them as they pass by.

Alongside this porch, symmetry and post-and-valance detailing define the smaller entry porch, framing its entrance from the walkway and making it clear that this is the way in. But because the main house door is set perpendicular to the street, the entry porch feels sheltered and private as well.

This unusual pairing of porches with complementary gable roofs and crisp white trim now completely distinguishes the front elevation of the once-homely house.

Triple corner posts and a capped kneewall create a semiprivate setting on a porch that is highly visible, yet can be reached only from inside the home.

A gracious main door with a wood-inlay design, sidelights, and transom can't be seen from the sidewalk, but because it's necessary to pause inside the entry porch, visitors get to appreciate its detailing.

Though the entry portal is small, it's spacious enough to shelter visitors. The space allows for an easy transition from private to public areas without an abrupt change.

CHAPTER 2

The Porch and the House

The American porch has evolved from the most primitive lean-to attached to a log cabin to a veritable outdoor room complete with comfy sofa, wet bar, and cozy rug underfoot. As our lifestyles (and our architecture) have grown more complex, so too have our porches, including the way we use them; they're less utilitarian today than they once were, and much more a reflection of how we spend our leisure time. They're not just for shucking corn anymore.

There was a period in American history when porches were everywhere. From the frenetic energy of a Queen Anne porch to the laid-back, tree-limb porch on a rustic Adirondack camp, porches were a part of who we were and how we lived. Our love for porches was so intense for a time (between the middle of the 19th and 20th centuries) that if you somehow ended up with a home that had no porch, you added one posthaste.

Traditional farmhouses were built with the climate and site in mind. A classic brick farmhouse nestles into the land; its wraparound porch built on sturdy piers provides easy access to the cellar.

Porches were a farmhouse constant, but the fancy front porch looked vastly different from the utilitarian porch in back. Fluted columns with capitals greeted visitors in front, whereas the back porch was often a messy extension of the kitchen.

The porch is an architectural mainstay of farmhouses, reflecting the vernacular building styles of every region in the country—from the traditional Northeast to the relaxed Southwest. In Massachusetts, for example, a farmhouse porch might be constructed of white clapboard and trimmed with simple colonial brackets. In the hills of North Carolina, it might be built off the ground on brick piers, facing the tobacco barn. In the Midwest, a sweeping wraparound porch might envelop a modest farmhouse, providing protection on the wide open prairie.

On farms everywhere, porches served as transition spaces between dusty, muddy fields and the clean rooms where families ate, slept, and gathered. In the same way that most homes had public rooms such as parlors in front and more informal rooms in back, porches were assigned activities. Most farmhouses had both front and back porches, serving two distinct functions. Situated off the kitchen, the back porch was where serious, messy work was done—from taking off muddy boots to plucking chickens. As such, the back porch was often plain and simple in its detailing. The front porch was usually more adorned and furnished with benches or rockers; the front porch was where the family went to "set a while" after the chores were done.

The changing face of the American porch

Over the years, many things have influenced porch styles in this country from climate and affluence to our penchant for adornment. These days, it is our love of nostalgia that is bringing back the traditional porch.

If there is a doyenne of American porches, it's the Greek Revival, with its generous proportions, soaring columns, and graceful lines. Often found in the South in the early- to mid-19th century, this porch had two purposes:

There's nothing shy or retiring about the Greek Revival, and its porches. Frequently found in the South, these porches had soaring columns that clearly elevated the status of the house—and its owners—in the eyes of visitors.

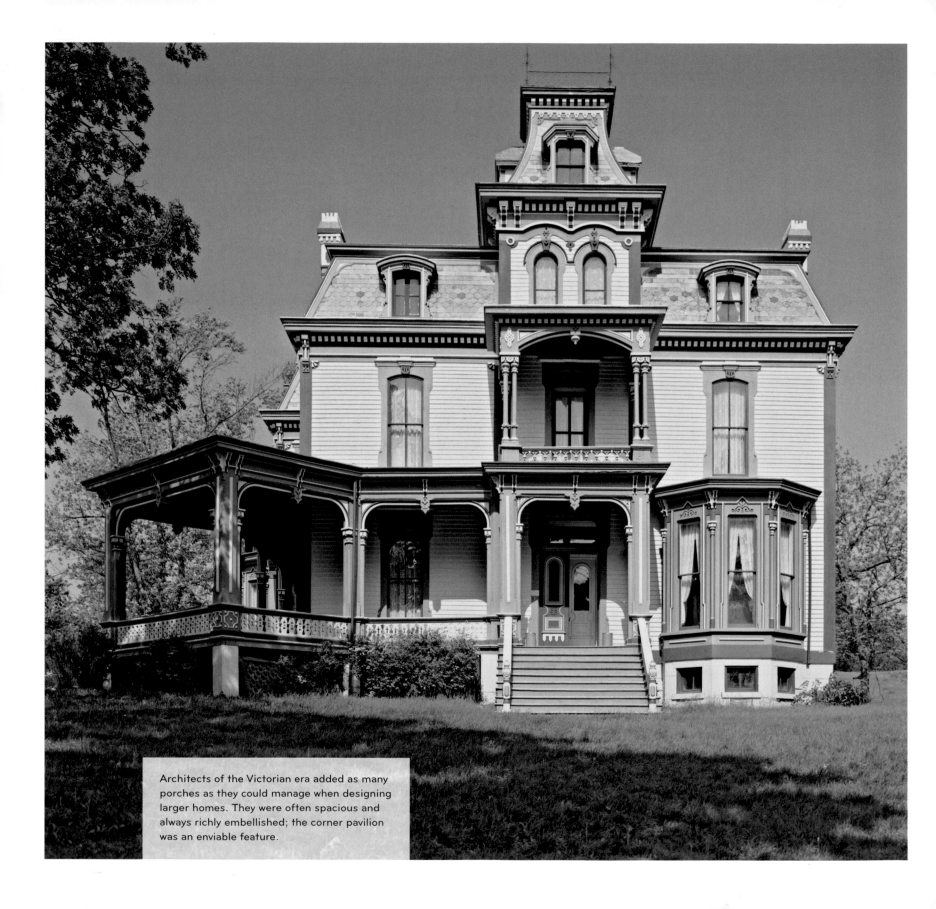

Architects of the Victorian era added as many porches as they could manage when designing larger homes. They were often spacious and always richly embellished; the corner pavilion was an enviable feature.

to shade the walls of the house from relentless heat and to put the wealth of the homeowner on very public display.

More modest (but no less distinctive) porches were built by European colonists imitating architectural styles found at home, and later by newly minted Americans bent on establishing styles all their own. The neocolonial is a case in point: It looks and "feels" traditional, but is usually altered in some way to suit more contemporary tastes.

French settlers in Louisiana and other parts of the South built stucco-sided homes with expansive elevated and two-story porches that often served as passageways in place of interior halls. Inspired by lessons learned in tropical colonies, the elevated porches on French colonial homes caught breezes and offered protection from floods. In New Orleans, the second-story balconies were dressed up with elaborate wrought iron railings.

Cool adobe homes covered with curved clay tiles protected Spanish colonists from the oppressive heat in California and parts of the Southwest. Some of their homes featured ground-level porches with shed roofs, whereas others had second-story covered balconies cantilevered out over the street or an interior courtyard.

From the beginning of the Victorian era in the late 1830s, the porch has been a defining feature of all Victorian house styles. Homes built in the Queen Anne style often had porches encircling the full first floor, while Second Empire homes had "pavilions" that projected off the main porch. Often, one porch wasn't enough; many homes had porches off the bedrooms on the second floor and even off the gables of the third floor as well. Victorian porches were highly embellished and painted in broad color palettes to accentuate the complexity of their details. The lavish decora-

Spread wide across the front of French colonial homes, sprawling porches—open, yet shaded by ample overhangs—were raised up to protect the first floor from seasonal flooding.

Spanish style homes had integrated porches with shed roofs covered with curved clay tiles. They often looked out onto interior courtyards.

Far from the grandeur of affluent towns, tiny porches were built onto even primitive houses hidden away in the woods.

tions that filled the inside of Victorian homes often spilled out onto their porches; in summer they might include rugs, fine furniture, and the best table settings.

The porch became an important feature of vacation homes as Americans came to enjoy more leisure time during and after the Industrial Revolution. Well-to-do families escaped the crowds and pollution of cities by spending summers in Shingle-style homes built along the coast, and no such home was without at least one porch. Many had porches tucked into a gable roof or under a second-story projection to capture views. Even modest beach cottages sported tiny covered entries just large enough to provide shelter from the elements. Inland, rustic Adirondack camps were adorned with porches made from trunk posts and twisted limb rails.

Arts and Crafts lovers championed a simpler style of architecture at the turn of the 20th century. The movement emerged as a reaction to the fussy Victorian period, but interestingly, the porch wasn't thrown out with the architectural bathwater. Deep integral porches were a distinctive feature of the Craftsman bungalow, noted for exposed rafters and stone and wood pilasters supporting overhead beams.

Early modern architecture was not enamored of porches. Minimalist homes featured large, fixed-glass panes for windows and air conditioned interior spaces. In that context, the porch seemed unnecessary. But today more architects are recognizing the beauty (as well as the utility and cultural importance) of porches, and they're reinterpreting them for use in modern homes. Today's porches tend to be taller and larger, but more transparent and thus less visually heavy than the porches of yore.

The Craftsman bungalow wasn't complete without a porch; it was often sided with stone and featured tapered columns that supported gabled roofs with exposed rafters.

The porch is back—reinterpreted as a sleeker, taller, more open structure than it was in the past. Contemporary architects are finding creative ways to make the porch feel fresh and new.

The best way to make a porch feel at home on your home is to mirror architectural details. Highly detailed post brackets echo and accentuate the arched shape of tall shuttered windows.

Adding the Perfect Porch to Your Home

Some houses look fine just as they are, but there aren't many that would *not* benefit from the addition of a porch. The question is, which porch? Luckily, it's not hard to figure out the answer. A house with strong architectural roots has a history to inspire you. There are house-plan collections and architectural reference books that can show you the most faithful way to add a porch onto your period house.

But what if you can't find your house in a history book? Then you need to take a close look to identify stylistic clues that can help you design a porch that looks like it belongs. Porch details—posts, rails, rooflines, eaves, and foundations—all have characteristics that can be designed to mirror the details on your home. Some details are so subtle that the average person won't notice them, such as the trim at the top of a porch post. In fact, there's any number of trim combinations that will work fine at the top of that post. But if you want to accurately match your new porch to your home, you need to do your homework. To make the new porch fit your old home, you'll need to consider elements that will guide your design: materials, proportion, and details.

Materials

Choosing materials that match (or are sympathetic to) an existing structure is fairly straightforward. Although some houses don't leave much room for creativity (a Romanesque home is one of the few that calls for an all-stone porch, for example), a great many porches are made of wood or some combination of wood and other materials.

How do you piece together those combinations? Get ideas from your house and its surrounding materials, including window trim, roofing,

A good porch follows the form of a house that has an identifiable style; it doesn't try to make it over. Scalloped shingles suggest Victorian inspiration, which is echoed in curved brackets and gently turned balusters and posts.

Good proportions are inherently pleasing to look at. A long porch built at grade sits comfortably on the land because so many square posts anchor its considerable roof. The structure's great size is checked by its low balustrade and closeness to the ground.

walkways, even outbuildings. As you'll see in the next chapter on porch anatomy, there are ample opportunities to introduce a mix of materials. The trick is to duplicate or complement the materials that have already been used to build and trim out your home. If the real thing (antique brick, for example) is no longer available, you can come close with reproduction materials and even synthetics, which we'll discuss in detail in Chapter 3.

Proportion

Of the three elements of good design, the most ethereal is proportion. It's the thing that most people don't consciously notice, but many know instinctively if it is wrong. On a porch, it might be the size or shape of the posts, rails, or trim. The best way to understand the effect that proportion has on design is to study porches that you like and don't like.

There are many reasons why a porch may appear unattractive to you, including color or a poor choice of materials, but a porch with bad proportions (columns that are poorly placed or too thin) will always feel awkward no matter how many times you paint it. When designing your own porch or reviewing your architect's design, remember that if it doesn't look right on paper, chances are it won't look good in person. If you can't tell by looking at plans, build a model to get a different perspective. In our practice, we build models of almost all of our projects, including porches.

Details

It's hard to separate details from proportion, because every detail has its own proportion and all are part of the porch as a whole. Details may include the rhythm of crown molding or the shape of a wooden decorative

Conspicuous details such as gingerbread trim make it easy to connect a porch and its house. A balustrade's unique cutout pattern is repeated on the gable, as well as on the balcony above the porch.

bracket. One way to determine if the details you've selected will work is to nail up samples during construction so you can see how they look.

Keep in mind that some details are for decorative purposes, whereas others play a critical role in the longevity of the porch. An overly ornate balustrade on a plain porch will stand out like a sore thumb, but a handrail that's joined to a post incorrectly might invite water into the structure, beginning the decline of the porch or even the foundation of the house itself.

A Good Fit

Have you ever looked at a house and sensed that something about it wasn't quite right? Perhaps it didn't look finished or feel balanced. Was it the placement of the windows? The pitch of the roof? The size of the porch? It's not always easy to put your finger on what's wrong, but it helps if you understand a few principles of good design. These drawings illustrate the difference between porches that are appropriately placed and in good proportion to the house—and those that aren't.

1. a) How awkward a big, boxy house looks with a microscopic portico attached.

b) How a house and porch are balanced when they are in proportion.

2. a) How skimpy columns from undersized lumber can make a porch look tacked on.

b) How a wide header and substantial columns appear to support a façade.

BEFORE **Too Tall and Ill-Defined Entry**

AFTER **Porch Balances Façade and Defines Main Entry**

BEFORE

Skimpy Columns

AFTER

Better Scale, Proportions, and Detailing

Big Moves Out Back

An awkward L-shape at the rear of the house (far left) was dramatically changed by replacing the deck with a breakfast room, at right, and adding a connecting porch that steps down, first to a patio, then the yard.

BEFORE

A North Carolina spec home with a nondescript rear elevation was sorely in need of usable outdoor living space.

An outdoor room with an indoor presence, the porch proper is finished with a beadboard ceiling, crown molding, upholstered chairs, a gas grill, and transomed French doors leading into the breakfast room.

AFTER

This transformation was nothing short of remarkable. The large-scale renovation included an enclosed breakfast room connected to a new covered porch complete with skylights, ceiling fans, and a brick fireplace. The new "keeping room" opens out to the porch through twin French doors that flank the wood-burning fireplace. Defined by traditional wood columns and handrails on two open sides, the porch mixes materials seamlessly; the floor is paved with natural stone and edged with rowlock brick that matches the original house. The ceiling is stained beadboard; a copper-clad roof features two large skylights that bathe the space with sunshine during the day. A 6-ft.-wide brick stairway leads down to a brick-paved patio and beyond to the gardens and yard. (Architect: Miller Nicholson, MNM Architects, Charlotte, N.C.)

The Transforming Porch

The lessons we've learned over hundreds of years of porch building in the United States should not be lost. Historical porches have endured because they were built to properly shed water, avoid rot, and withstand the elements. They possess timeless beauty because proportions were carefully considered and they were designed in harmony with the houses to which they were attached.

A well-made, but too-small, porch might last for a hundred years, but it will always look like a mistake. We believe it's important to give very careful thought to the design and construction of porches—just as our ancestors did.

As we've seen, it's not hard to know what kind of porch to build if your house is of a distinctive style, era, or pedigree. But what if your house has no distinctive style to speak of? What if it's really nothing more than a Plain Jane ranch, colonial, or Cape? Well, it's not as bad as you think—not if you consider the porch's amazing ability to transform the look of a home.

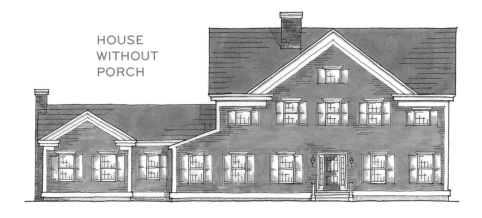

HOUSE WITHOUT PORCH

HOUSE WITH PORCH

A Builder's Colonial Gets Personality

BEFORE

A nondescript 1960s build-er's colonial in Mendham, a quaint pedestrian community in northern New Jersey, pos-sessed unrealized potential.

The porch took the lead, but there were many improvements made to the façade, including the installation of larger windows and new siding and trim in a cohesive sage-and-white color palette.

A stone foundation, tapered wood columns, and a sheltering overhang lend the new porch its Craftsman-like appeal. The design was reinforced by repeating the gable overhead.

AFTER

A spacious 10-ft. by 14-ft. Craftsman-inspired porch replaced the clumsy, faux Greek Revival portico that no one ever used. Although the basic shape of the house wasn't altered, new details redefined it, notably the low-pitched porch roof (repeated above on the second story, and again over the garage). Dark-stained shingle siding replaced the former patchwork of brick, shingles, and shutters. On the porch, tapered columns, white wood brackets, and smooth river stone combine to take the house from boring to beautiful. Surrounded by an ever-changing perennial garden, the sheltering, south-facing porch is now a favorite gathering place for family. (Architect: Karen M. Duncan Bonner, OBL Architects, Chester, N.J.)

A portico that didn't fool anyone, the former entry to the home was an ill-proportioned afterthought to this cookie-cutter colonial.

Let your porch take the lead

For the simple reason that a porch is so visible and open to interpretation, it can actually define the style of a house that has none to begin with. A case in point: We were recently paid a visit by clients who had bought a home on an idyllic, tree-lined country road. They told us the house was too small for their family, but more important, they just didn't like the way it looked. We rode over with them to take a look and immediately agreed that the house seemed to lack character. In fact, it was about as plain as any home we'd ever been asked to renovate. (See "About Face" on p. 76).

Among other changes, we proposed a wraparound porch that included a private deck off two second-story bedrooms. The porch alone made a palpable difference in the way the house looked—and the way the owners looked at the house. They liked the view from the porch so much they decided to clear additional land to enhance it. In turn, they found they were spending more time outdoors. In this case, the porch not only transformed the house, but also inspired the owners and altered the surrounding landscape.

This doesn't mean that you can work magic on your house or your lifestyle by simply adding a porch you like. As with any addition, you must consider the existing structure, materials, proportions, details—all the things that make for a seamless transformation.

Rediscovering a Porch from the Past

1915–1949

Space is at a premium in a small house, and most of us, given the choice between interior and exterior room, would choose the former. But North Carolina architect John Phares and his wife Elizabeth opted to give up square footage in favor of restoring the original porch to their 1916 bungalow.

The couple decided to research the history of their little home a few years back with the intention of restoring it—faithfully—in accordance with the North Carolina State Historic Preservation Office.

They knew the house had been "updated" at least twice: The porch had been enclosed and a bay window added to the left of the front door. They tracked down photographs taken before the first remodel and were delighted to learn that a sweet shingled porch with arched openings had once graced the home.

The homeowners learned that they would have to use photographic documents (with only a few minor alterations) to make them eligible for a tax credit. They corrected proportions a bit and made the new porch 10 ft. deep instead of 12 ft. deep, but even so, lost approximately 230 sq. ft. of heated indoor space. They found wood shingles that matched those shown in a pre-1940s photo. They calculated the exact curve and spring point of the arches on the three open sides to recreate the look of the original porch exactly.

The process of reclaiming the long-lost porch was costly and time consuming, but the Phareses don't regret a minute of it. The modest bungalow has enriched the streetscape, pleased the neighbors, and provided the couple with a deep sense of satisfaction.

1949 1975

TODAY

Open Land Inspires a Country Home

BEFORE

Uncomfortably perched on a quiet country lane, this house cried out for a stronger connection with the land.

AFTER

A deep, open wraparound porch allowed the house to embrace the fields surrounding it. To punctuate the long span of the roof and bring additional light into the rooms off the porch, an open gable was added over the entry. The sweeping porch includes a "hidden" deck off the bedrooms on the second floor, from which the homeowners can enjoy panoramic views of their open land and the stream that flows beyond. (Architect: James M. Crisp, AIA, Millbrook, N.Y.)

A fresh coat of white paint and a classic wraparound porch literally changed the essence of the little pink house that sat in a picturesque meadow.

Gone is the severe fence that bordered the home; the new open porch invites family members to actually use the comfortable space for sitting and dining.

Drama in a Minneapolis Backyard

An informal entry was vastly improved when a striking black-stained porch was added to the rear of a relatively nondescript brick home. With an unusual screening pattern and contemporary feel, the porch single-handedly updates the hip-roofed city house.

BEFORE

A massive red brick home in Minneapolis lacks definition and a comfortable everyday entry from the backyard.

AFTER

The simple screened-in porch is open and airy, yet in pleasing proportion to the 2½-story house. The porch structure is substantial and "thick," with 14-in. corner columns and 8-in. walls throughout. The boxy space is made more dynamic by alternating the placement of the screens. They were installed outside the porch wall in the middle sections and inside the porch wall at the corners. This subtle move created a practical inside ledge while reinforcing the sturdiness of the posts that define the porch. For dramatic effect, all porch surfaces were stained black except the contrasting tongue-and-groove floor and ceiling, which were finished in clear cedar. (Architect: Paul Buum, SALA, Minneapolis, Minn.)

How a porch can redirect traffic

The extent to which a porch can change the patterns of your daily life should not be underestimated. When a porch is added to a home, its impact is felt immediately. The visual impression it makes is clear from the yard or the street, but a porch affects flow patterns in and around the home as well.

An outdated tract house in Tulsa, OK, is a case in point (see photo below). A respectful renovation resulted in a simplified floor plan and the addition of front and back porches that gave the formerly nondescript house a heightened sense of importance. But what is perhaps more notable is how the new porches changed the way the homeowners used their backyard. The new rear porch and patio are now "destinations" that inspired the installation of winding brick walkways that direct traffic around the side of the home to the yard. What had been stark, seldom-used space is now a multi-level, multi-use entertaining haven for the family. Brick pavers lead down to a courtyard, fountain and formal dining area. The homeowners appreciate the ease with which they now move from house through the yard, encouraging them to spend more time outdoors.

Because a new porch can actually allow you to direct the way people experience the area around your home, we often take advantage of that opportunity when we design for our clients. We spend a lot of time

The backyard of this dime-a-dozen suburban home was transformed by the addition of a gently elevated brick patio and porch. Anchored by two sets of defining posts at the corners and artfully lit by sconces and spots, the new space inspires gracious entertaining.

thinking about access; we look at all the possible configurations of doors and windows onto a porch, knowing that those decisions will affect both circulation and furniture placement inside and out. For example, you can ease traffic indoors—at least some of the time, depending on the weather —by adding a door to either end of a long porch. You can make a grand entrance even grander by designing a wide porch stair that unmistakably greets guests and directs them to the door. And you can create a brand new

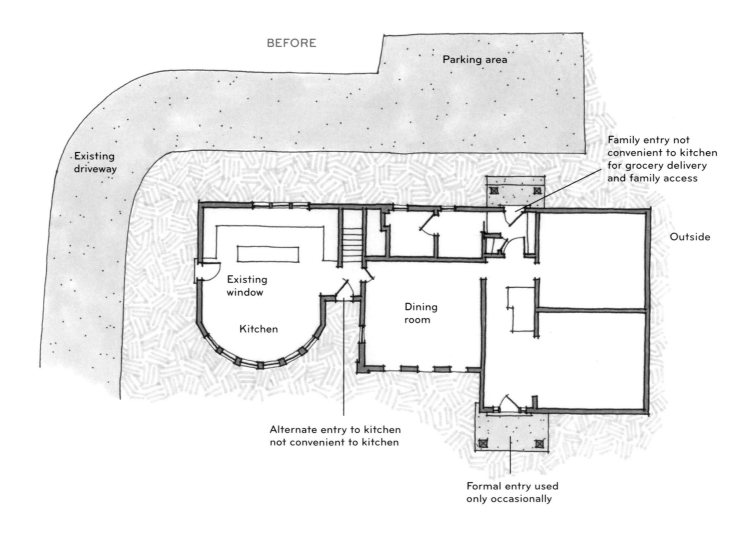

BEFORE

Parking area

Existing driveway

Family entry not convenient to kitchen for grocery delivery and family access

Existing window

Outside

Kitchen

Dining room

Alternate entry to kitchen not convenient to kitchen

Formal entry used only occasionally

circular path between two rooms if one already has a door to the outside: Picture a dining room with French doors that open onto a patio. Add a porch off the adjacent living room—and open up the wall between the rooms.

Sometimes a client wants to add a porch that can potentially pose problems. It may block views or intersect the second story in a way that interferes with windows. For one such client we solved a problem instead. We

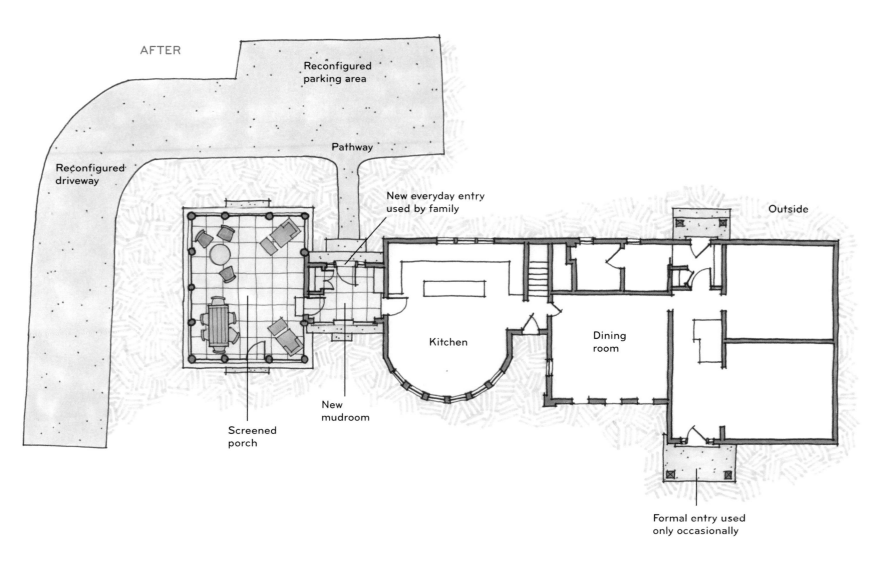

Even a large porch can be affordable if it's designed without frills. Exposed rafters and the plainest of post-and-rail systems can keep costs down while contributing to a porch's simple elegance.

designed a good-size porch at one end of the house, along with a connector that doubles as an informal entry/mudroom to allow family members to enter conveniently into the kitchen, which they couldn't do before. This transition space changed circulation patterns and also gave the porch a little "breathing room."

Getting your money's worth

As you might expect, no porch is cheap to build, not even a small one. Most can cost tens of thousands of dollars, but compared to any heated, finished space, a porch is a bargain.

In its simplest form, a porch needs a roof overhead and some columns to hold that roof up. Although an addition generally requires a full foundation, many porches only need piers. There are exceptions to that rule, of course, and we'll discuss those in the Chapter 3. Windows and interior doors always run up the cost of new rooms, but for the most part they're not required when building a porch. An interior finished space needs insulation, heating and/or cooling systems, extensive electrical service, and finishes, but a porch doesn't. Granted, a porch may involve other costly modifications to your home (new windows or doors, paths, walkways, and landscaping), but we still think that overall a porch is a good deal. Where else can you get comfort, space, good looks, and an improved floor plan, inside and out? Talk about home improvement!

Two Points of View

The new screened porch is quite spacious and in proportion to the rest of the house. By adding the open-air room to the bumped-out entry at the rear, the homeowners created a comfortable nook for a patio.

BEFORE

A small house, circa 1925, on an untamed lot in semirural North Carolina cries out for privacy, a porch, and a patio.

Wood slats on one side of the porch effectively conceal the less appealing views of a dog run and neighboring house.

AFTER

The owners/architects designed a screened porch and trellis that gave the backyard a much-needed identity and helped to enhance one view while blocking another. Two sides of the porch are open to the garden, a new patio, and steps that lead to a small but lush lawn. The third side of the porch was fitted with slats to filter the view of the owners' dog run as well as the neighbor's house, which is very close by. The slats are reminiscent of those used in area tobacco barns to allow breezes to flow through. With a beadboard ceiling left natural, cedar columns, and redwood slats, the porch serves as a "summer room," whereas the trellised patio, warmed by fires on cool evenings, is where the homeowners enjoy spending time in spring and fall. (Architects: Dieatra Blackburn, AIA, and Betsy West, AIA, Studio 1 Architects, PC, Charlotte, N.C.)

A Walk on the Wild Side

They say location is everything, and that's certainly true

Baton Rouge,
Louisiana

for Steve and Mary Kay, whose dream house sits on a lot that backs up to the Bayou Duplantier, a wetland paradise filled with lush greenery, wildlife, and extraordinary views. What's amazing is that the property, a little under an acre, is located right in the middle of the city of Baton Rouge.

"The area brought back memories of older, active neighborhoods with children riding bikes and people walking," says Mary Kay. "We fell in love with the lot when we realized that it sloped off to meet the wetlands."

Built in 1958, the original house—a suburban hip-roofed ranch—was too small for the couple's growing family and didn't take full advantage of its natural surroundings. It also lacked a street presence and strong entry, so the couple knew they had to give thoughtful consideration to the renovation.

Because they had recently vacationed out West in a mountain lodge and found the experience so relaxing and enjoyable, they decided they wanted

In this view from the backyard, well-proportioned columns do more than support the roof. They define boundaries where the porch opens up to the yard and the lawn falls gracefully away.

(facing page) The new front-entry porch both invites and protects. Its pleasing symmetry and dignified profile provide an open welcome. Because it never rains but it pours in Louisiana, the porch's substantial size offers ample coverage overhead.

(above left) The porch is spacious enough to allow for a few potted plants and a chair, making it a comfortable vantage point from which to survey the street.

(above right) Rustic and textural, the rear-porch columns have a rhythmic repetition that lends interest to the otherwise open porch. Note how the architect used the strength of brick piers to tie the tapered wood columns to the ground.

(right) Because this side of the house is visible to the street, the walkway and landscaping were designed to build anticipation as visitors approach.

Craftsman touches on the porch are classic. Architect-designed gas lights provide a soft glow and old-fashioned ambience to evening get-togethers on the porch. The natural cedar details of the rafters, posts, beams, and ceiling connect purposefully with the cedar shingles on the house. The clerestory window feature on the exterior of the roof brings light onto the porch.

to recreate that feeling at home. They asked their architect, Kevin Harris of Baton Rouge, if he could help them capture a similar rustic sensibility and connection with the great outdoors. Thus, porches became a very important part of the project.

First, Harris gave the rambling house character by designing a new roofline. He then rearranged the interior of the home, switching the living room—where family members spend most of their time—with the dining room, which offered a better view.

He then designed a new entry porch facing the road in front and a new entertaining porch at the rear, both tailored to create smooth transitions indoors and out. The tall porches have a distinctive Craftsman-like quality, with exposed, rough-sawn rafters and substantial wood columns on brick bases that define the structures at a distance.

In front, the porch establishes a dominant entry, giving the house a clear sense of style and a new feeling of importance. In back, three sets of French doors extend the home's living space by opening onto the generous new porch and beyond, across the lawn and into the backyard.

The family uses the back porch all the time. On rainy weekends, the porch provides a respite from the drone of television shows; it's a great place to sit quietly, listening to the splash of the rain on the roof. The new porch has done duty as a reviewing stand and an outdoor kitchen.

It's also a great place for thinking things through. Says Mary Kay, "My husband and I make all of our important decisions on the rear porch since it's where we can get away from the rest of the family and the telephones for a moment of solitude."

Tall French doors and clerestory windows transfer interior light to the sheltered back porch. The view inside is impeccably balanced; even paintings on the far wall are hung so they can be seen clearly through the doors.

A Tale of Two Stories

The Hanlon house is located on an original land grant

in rural Harford County, Md., known for horses and foxhunts. It's surrounded by more than 10,000 acres of farmland and preserved open space.

For much of the 20th century the Hanlon property, along with an intact but quite derelict circa-1870 house, went without notice. But in 1997, a semiretired couple from Pennsylvania, both active members of the local hunt club, purchased the property for the purpose of preserving open land. At first they thought they'd build a new home, but they were taken with the straightforward simple charm of the existing house, as was their son, architect Rob Kinsley. They knew they needed more room and flexible space for entertaining, but they vowed to bring the house back to life.

Although the renovation did substantially increase the size of the early farmhouse, the distinction between old and new is subtle, thanks in part to the defining two-story porch on the east side and a smaller, reconstructed terrace porch on the west side.

One porch, many spatial experiences. Underneath, the motor court serves as an entry-level foundation, while keeping large garage doors in check. The main porch extends the living room and then flows out to an open terrace. The upper porch offers both a protected, private retreat and a sunny, open deck.

The connections are seamless between the original house and its new wing, as well as between the house and the porch.

The porch door, a detail found typically on houses located farther south, punctuates the transition from the "inside/outside" porch to the terrace, which is unequivocally outdoors.

A substantial addition to the original house hides behind the detailed porch. An integrated stone retaining wall and supporting stone piers give the impression that the porch has always been there.

Parties, Privacy, and Views

The two-story porch can best be described as a hybrid: It's designed for entertaining, for privacy—and for views. It's built on two levels with exposed structural piers below.

On the main level, the renovation called for a large gathering space augmented by a wide sitting porch. French doors between the two graciously facilitate traffic in and out of the house, and because the porch faces the entrance drive, it welcomes visitors as they draw near. Flowing out of the new gathering room, the open, detail-rich elevation helps scale down the addition, while allowing the home to retain its country character.

With French doors thrown open, the first-floor porch provides an ideal transition from the inside, out. The homeowners wanted an accessible, adaptable space that would grow comfortably to accommodate guests.

The covered second-story porch creates a master bedroom annex of sorts, extending the private realm to the great outdoors.

The architect says it's the perfect place for a party or a casual, light lunch, it's also his parents' favorite spot for morning coffee when they're at the house alone.

The upper level combines a sheltered, private retreat for the master suite with a sunny, open area that connects to the side of the house.

The lower level cleverly disguises the basement garage, forming a motor court. Stone piers echo the original foundation and the retaining wall that creates a boundary for the a side terrace. The stone anchors the porch, grounding the house and giving it a sense of belonging on the site.

One of the more interesting features of this porch is its side door, leading from the main level down to an open brick terrace. The homeowners were enamored of porch doors often found on homes in the South and asked that the detail be included. The door provides a clear point of entry and enhances both the porch and the terrace by defining their boundaries and giving them a heightened sense of place.

A much-smaller porch sits on the opposite side of the house. The modest original was restored and refreshed, complete with an aged brick floor and an Arts and Crafts–inspired swing. Accessible from the living room and dining room, this porch has an informal feel but is elegant in its simplicity. At grade level, it flows directly into the landscape and is as much a part of the garden as it is the house. Situated street side, it's a transitional porch, buffering the public and the private—the inside and the outside—and providing a comfortable meeting place for all.

Railing detail repeats the design of the porches. This simple touch ties all the spaces together into a cohesive whole.

Old Meets New in the Maryland Hills

The Hanlon homestead is steeped in history, so it was important to the homeowners that the renovation not make the house feel garishly new. The architect took pains to integrate the old and the new. Rooflines flow into one another, with eave heights on the old sections repeated on the new. The clapboard siding was copied on the new sections, including the gable end over the east porch. Small gable windows repeat from the existing structure to the new. And though the porch rails and columns are new, they are detailed to reference the scale and simple lines of the original home. Built-up post caps lend a little personality to the straightforward square balusters and basic bottom rail.

Columns at the corners define the space, provide a sense of enclosure, and frame the views beyond.

Double-post detailing is carried throughout, on both the main and upper porches. Visually substantial, the posts evoke a sense of security and comfort and reassurance that they will stand the test of time.

Stonesthrow from the Past

This early-20th-century lakeside retreat was purchased

as a weekend home, even though it is only a half hour away from where the owners, Michael and Lynn Guerriero, live in New Jersey (hence its name, "Stonesthrow").

The property appealed to the couple because they didn't want to spend precious weekend time commuting, says Lynn, but the house was clearly in need of renovating. Although the old place had its charms (a fieldstone veneer first floor and an east-side open porch), it had its downside, too (vinyl siding and three small bedrooms).

The couple wanted more room for their children and grandchildren, and a house that would lend itself to outdoor entertaining. What guided the renovation, says Michael, was a desire for a home that would look completely original, nestled comfortably into its wooded lot.

Surrounded by woods and furnished with wicker, this porch is the perfect getaway for a weekend home. It's spacious enough to accommodate a variety of sitting areas, yet feels homey thanks to finishing touches like rugs, pillows, flowers, and warm overhead lighting.

This small porch on the east side was screened in after the new porch was added. The stone veneer on the main house was left exposed, lending texture and reinforcing the inside/outside nature of the space.

Indoors, their wish list included a conversion of the attic into a master suite. Outdoors, they wanted a new entertaining/dining porch that would be accessible from the kitchen and afford a view toward the lake. They also wanted the east-side porch screened in.

Bringing the Indoors Out

The new porch features substantially proportioned square columns and striking mahogany detailing: railings, tongue-and-groove decking, and beadboard ceilings. Repeating the existing stone veneer, the porch foundations are made of fieldstone collected from the property.

Furnished with wicker, twig furniture, rugs, sconces, and buckets of flowers, the long, homey porch has a decidedly indoor feel. It connects to the kitchen and the living room through new windows and French doors. For cross-ventilation and easy traffic flow, a door at the other end of the living room opens to the screened porch. The Guerrieros eat most of their meals out on the porch, even when the weather is less than perfect. They once seated guests at a long table on the porch, hosting a wine tasting for 40.

Look overhead for the bonus room: The idea for a new sun porch came while construction of the dining porch was underway. Deemed quite desirable by the homeowners, the cozy sun porch was made part of the dining-porch roof. Now sunlight filters through reclaimed stained-glass windows into the stairwell leading up to the master bedroom suite in the old attic.

New landscaping features include a fieldstone retaining wall, flagstone walks around the house and down to the lake, a gazebo, and a terrace fitted with a fire pit off the screened porch. By mirroring the natural materials used to build the original house, the new (and improved) porches look as though they have always belonged.

Color and contrasting materials give this porch comfort appeal. Sizable square posts stand at intervals along the striking mahogany balustrade. Other mahogany details include tongue-and-groove decking and a beadboard ceiling.

This porch is so sheltering that the homeowners rest, read, play games, and eat most of their meals out there, even when the weather is less than perfect. Serious furniture (no resin picnic sets here) gives the outdoor space a true, indoor, furnished feel.

More than anything, the homeowners wanted their home to look original and completely at home on the wooded lot tucked comfortably into the land, shaded by nearby trees.

CHAPTER 3

The Anatomy of a Porch

There comes a time in the planning process when it becomes clear that the whole of your porch is much more than the sum of its parts. Ironically, it happens just when you begin to think about your project in terms of its individual components. Sometimes the selection of a key element, like a railing or floor, can put the entire project into perspective. Early on the choices may overwhelm you; it can be daunting to have to decide everything from foundation type and floor finish to step width and railing style.

Remember that every choice you make should be a function of the overall design, how you plan to use your porch, and your location and climate. Your ultimate goal should be a functional and beautiful porch that complements the exterior and interior of your home and is constructed in such a way that it gracefully weathers the seasons for years to come.

The many parts and pieces of a porch contribute to its overall look and function.

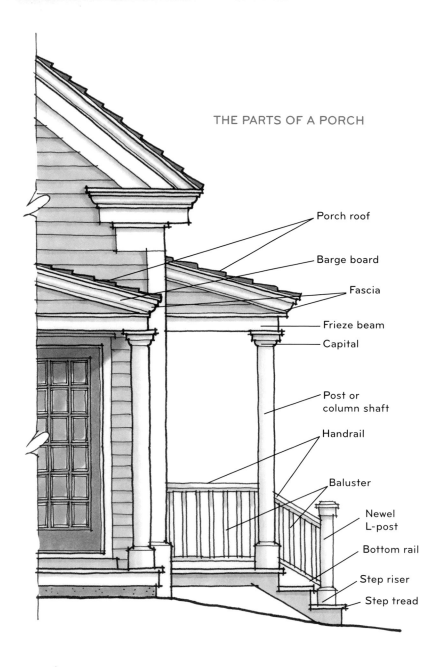

THE PARTS OF A PORCH

Porch roof

Barge board

Fascia

Frieze beam

Capital

Post or
column shaft

Handrail

Baluster

Newel
L-post

Bottom rail

Step riser

Step tread

How do you get there? First, understand that the decision process isn't linear. Every decision can (and should) affect another. You may start out down one path but discover that a choice you make midway through the process forces you to backtrack. What happens when you fall in love with a highly embellished balustrade that doesn't jibe with the brick flooring you selected weeks ago? It may mean going back to the drawing board. Trust us, it's far better to work hard at creating a style palette at this stage than to look at a badly mismatched porch for years to come.

In this chapter we take a closer look at the parts of every porch, from the basics to the finishing touches. We offer up some food for thought that will help you make good choices and take your porch plan to the next level.

Foundations: Starting from the Ground Up

A strong foundation is absolutely essential to the long life of any porch. The region you live in and the slope of your building site will influence the kind of foundation you choose, but there's a good reason why nearly every foundation is dug deep below ground level. In some areas, frost heave can be an awesome force, and the only way to protect your porch from serious damage is to place your footings below the frost line. This prevents the foundation from moving when the soil expands and contracts as it freezes and thaws during the colder months. In other regions, the soil may be too swampy to support the weight of a porch, so pilings must be dug deep enough to hit solid ground. How far you need to dig (usually between 36 in. and 48 in.) is determined by several factors—and these are quite different in northern Minnesota than they are in southern Florida.

Steep slopes

If your house is sited on a steep slope, chances are this is a great opportunity to create a scenic overlook. But a porch here most likely will require foundation piers or tall walls, highly visible elements that should be considered in the overall design. The total load exerted on each pier (as well as budget constraints) will often determine what materials you choose. For long

Foundations should be strong first and style-appropriate second. The porch on a rustic weekend home was constructed of recycled split logs found on the property.

Code Compliance and Why It Matters

Think you don't need a light on your porch? Think again. In most jurisdictions, electrical codes mandate that lighting be installed near all exterior doors so guests (and residents) can come and go safely at night. Building codes regulate everything from weight load and footing depth to the required clearance to overhead wires. Railing height, stairway width, the distance between balusters, and the dimensions of risers and treads all must comply.

Why the need for these guidelines? To keep people from falling off your porch, and to keep your porch from falling down. Your architect and contractor should be familiar with requirements in your area, but it wouldn't hurt to double-check with them to be sure that your porch will, in fact, be "up to code."

A sprawling wrap-around porch needs extra support. Lattice panels lighten the look of heavy concrete piers and keep air circulating under the porch to prevent mold.

spans carrying heavy loads, steel beams and posts may be the way to go. For lighter loads, you may prefer wood, which is easy to work with, readily available, and often less expensive than steel. Masonry piers are another option.

On a steep slope, the entire foundation (including bracing elements and connections) should be engineered not only for porch load, but for climate and soil and geologic conditions.

Steep slopes can be a challenge to build on, but sometimes they inspire creative solutions. Tall piers enhance the view and complement the stark contemporary style of a pavilion overlooking a river.

105

In some climates, humidity and the threat of flooding demand that porches be placed as far off the ground as possible. Surrounding shade trees offer a respite from the hot summer sun.

Whenever you build on a sloped site there will be appreciable space between the ground and the main porch floor. This found space can be a welcome asset; simply add flooring and you can use it as a terrace. It can open to the lower level of the house or be accessed by stairs from the porch above. It can even serve as a storage area.

Flat sites or gentle slopes

A flat or gently sloped area allows you to build a porch at (or near) ground level, but that doesn't mean you can forgo foundation work. You'll still be attaching your porch in some manner to the structure of the main house, and if anything causes the porch to move, it can have a detrimental, if not disastrous, effect on your home.

When you build at grade level you can more easily work with substantial materials such as concrete, brick, or stone. And though you may think these materials are impervious to moisture, you almost can't do enough to protect your porch from water damage (see "Water is the Enemy" on p. 108). Your porch floor must be sloped to allow water to run off and not seep into stone grout or joints in the concrete. Proper sloping of the surrounding grade is also important to direct water away from both the porch and house foundations. We like to install perimeter drains at the base of any foundation to collect and direct water to another part of the property. Wood foundations close to grade need special attention. To prevent rot and mold, never completely enclose a foundation or impede airflow around it; cover it with a lattice or baluster-like skirting instead.

Skirting the Issue

A porch skirt is a decorative feature that starts at ground level and runs up to your porch floor, wrapping around the foundation and hiding the structural underpinnings of your porch from view. A porch skirt has an added advantage of keeping critters from setting up residence under your porch.

Cedar lattice is commonly used for skirts, and we especially like a heavier, 1-in.-thick lattice set in a square pattern. We find it holds up well to weather and provides a substantial look.

Although lattice is traditional, readily available, and easy to replace, there are other inspired skirting options to choose from. Many turn-of-the-century porches were wrapped with elaborate traditional saw and scrollwork panels made of wood. These fanciful skirt panels are being reproduced today, and though they do impart a period look, keep in mind they will require constant upkeep. Whatever skirt you choose, it's a good idea to build in a hinged or removable panel to provide easy access under the porch for maintenance.

When a porch is set at grade, weathered brick flooring can be laid alongside a neatly trimmed lawn. Smooth stone pillars stand in contrast to the rough texture of the brick.

Flooring: Creating a Platform

Once the foundation is established, it's time to consider the more visible parts of the porch, beginning with the floor. Much more than a surface to walk on, a floor sets the tone for your space. A painted wood floor, for example, says casual and country, whereas a stone or weathered brick floor feels more substantial and formal. Tile floors can run from rustic to ultrasophisticated, depending on tile size, color, and finish.

In most cases, at least part of your porch floor will be exposed to the elements, so the flooring is often vulnerable to blowing rains and snow.

Water Is the Enemy

Unless it's on ice with a twist of lemon, water is not a welcome guest on any porch. Water can damage flooring and promote mold growth on porch surfaces wherever it drips, puddles, or pools. The best solution is to keep water from ever reaching your porch, but failing that, you'll want to encourage it to leave as quickly as possible.

Here are some suggestions:

• Slope any exposed soil under the porch away from the center to direct water runoff.

• Cover exposed soil under the porch with a moisture barrier to reduce the upward migration of moisture.

• Encourage airflow beneath the porch by using ornamental vents or lattice skirting.

• Slope porch framing away from the house (anywhere from 1/8 in. to 1/4 in. per ft.).

• Run decking boards perpendicular to the main house to direct water away.

• Prime all sides, including cut edges, of all porch materials.

• Provide air access at the base and the top of all columns and newel posts to allow airflow up and around, to combat moisture that may get in.

• Add a bottom rail to balustrades to keep baluster ends above snow and rainwater runoff.

• Add a bevel to the top edge of the rail in one or both directions to further direct runoff.

• When caulking an intersection between two pieces of wood, use the best caulk available; we prefer one made of polyurethane.

Tile can often appear rustic, but when placed next to soaring stucco arches, finished white pavers have quite a sophisticated look.

The look of a traditional porch can be created with wood, which may need a strong protective finish like marine paint to keep it in good shape.

Although some materials and finishes hold up better than others, we always build floors on a slight slope in order to shed water. The slope can be as slight as ⅛ in. per ft., which is enough to prevent puddles but not enough to be felt underfoot.

Wood

Wood is probably the most traditional flooring material you can choose. Its use varies by region, with cypress readily available in the South and redwood more commonly found in the West. Fir has long been the preferred wood for traditional painted floors in the Northeast.

Installation is generally the same everywhere. Floorboards may be milled for tongue-and-groove applications, or boards may simply be installed side by side with the exposed edges rounded over.

Natural wood. We like fir flooring, but have noticed recently that new-growth fir isn't holding up as well as the denser, old-growth lumber we're accustomed to. Newer woods seem to require stronger protective finishes (including specially formulated deck paints, semitransparent decking stains, or clear synthetic or oil finishes) that must be scrupulously maintained.

A good fir alternative is mahogany, which provides longevity at an affordable price. Mahogany can be painted, but the choice of primer is important because mahogany has a resinous nature. This makes it more rot resistant than some other woods, but can affect its ability to take finishes well.

If you don't want to paint, consider a Brazilian import called ipe. This incredibly dense wood resists rot and insects, isn't prone to splitting, and is nearly impervious to the damaging effects of weather. Ipe doesn't require

The floors on wide-open porches take a beating in nearly any climate. Because they can be pounded by driving rain or bleached by the sun, special attention should be paid to materials and finishes.

A narrow overhang is often all you need to give visitors a place to keep dry.

finishing to maintain its integrity, and when exposed to the elements it colors to a soft gray. The downside is its hardness, which can dull router blades quickly, making it difficult to work with.

Treated wood. A cost-effective option is pressure-treated wood, but not all of these rot-resistant, chemically treated woods are approved for residential use. ACQ (Alkaline Copper Quaternary) is one treated wood that is acceptable, but it can be quite corrosive to screws and other fasteners, so you'll need to use more expensive stainless steel or hot-dip galvanized fasteners. Because some pressure-treated woods are prone to cupping, splitting, and shrinkage, manufacturers may recommend you

"Wood" without the Work

There isn't a porch enthusiast among us who wouldn't love a traditional wood floor that wasn't a pain to maintain. Today's synthetic flooring materials, though far from perfect, have provided an option many of us can live with. Most synthetics come in four or more colors and a variety of textures, ranging from smooth to coarse wood grain (though some "faux woods" are more convincing than others).

Synthetics require little maintenance and they last a long time. But there are a few compromises: They're usually more expensive than natural woods, they're heavier and harder to work with, and although synthetics have come a long way, they still don't look enough like the real thing to satisfy many homeowners.

Synthetic wood products fall into two general categories:

• **Wood and resin composites.** These products are manufactured under several names, including Trex® and "tendura". Because these composites do contain wood, there's no guarantee they will never absorb water and/or grow mold, especially if they are milled during the installation process.

• **Wood-free composites.** These completely wood-free synthetics are becoming more widely available, and are constantly being refined to weigh less, last longer, and resist mold. They're distributed as Bear Board™, Pro Cell, and CorrectDeck®.

Wood Flooring Patterns

You can add an extra design element to your wood flooring by laying the boards in creative ways—on the diagonal or in a geometric pattern (think parquet floor but with a larger pattern). Another option is to mix woods. One possibility: Lay the outside perimeter with ipe boards and fill the inside field with mahogany boards laid on the diagonal. Painted or not, wood floors are beautiful, and there's no reason why they have to be plain.

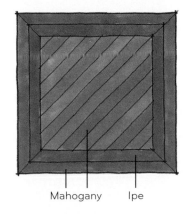

Mahogany   Ipe

Spiral pattern

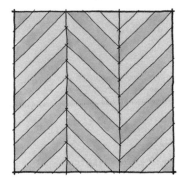

Herringbone pattern

wait a year before applying a finish. You can avoid this problem by selecting kiln-dried wood and then coating it with a water-protective finish such as paint or stain.

Masonry

Masonry makes a stunning porch floor, one with a substantial, almost organic feel. Weather resistant and virtually maintenance free, masonry floors have only two major drawbacks: Their weight may require reinforced foundations and they can be expensive. Your choices include the following:

Stone. Stone (including granite, bluestone, fieldstone, and slate) is available milled into rectangular shapes or in its natural, irregular state. We often use regular shapes along the perimeters of our porches and fill in the rest with irregular stones. This gives the edges a nice, clean line while the rest of the floor looks a bit more casual and relaxed. Stone is available in three finishes: *polished* (shiny and formal), *honed* (smooth and aged), and *flamed* (gritty and rustic).

Brick. Antique brick has a soft, mottled look that makes a lovely porch floor. Note, however, that not all reclaimed brick was meant to be used outdoors. Because they may have been fired at lower temperatures, many old bricks are prone to water absorption, which can result in spalling (layers breaking off) and cracking, especially in freezing temperatures. If you want the look of old brick with the advantages of modern materials, there are bricks on the market that are colored and tumbled to give them vintage appeal. Whether you are looking for a patina or a clean, consistent appearance, any well-stocked brickyard will provide a wide selection of bricks in many colors, shades, sizes, and textures.

Smooth stone can look textured but neat when it's milled into rectangular shapes and the grout lines are kept to a minimum. A casual and relaxed pattern is created by alternating shapes.

White concrete flooring is neatly scored on the diagonal to complete a clean, contemporary space that opens onto a crystal-clear pool and neatly trimmed lawn.

Tile

Tile (clay fired to a very high temperature) makes a durable porch floor with a cool, attractive, and low-maintenance finish. Consistently thick, machined tile has straight edges, which makes installation relatively easy. Handmade tile is irregular in thickness or shape (or both), making it more difficult and expensive to install. Whether machined or handmade, be sure the tile you choose is fired to stand up to the rigors of your climate. Glazing is an important consideration. Unglazed tile is more porous and so more prone to water damage and staining. Although glazed tile stains less, it can be slippery when wet. Keep in mind that most floor tiles do not come with shaped edges, so you may want to consider using a mix of materials, perhaps a border of thicker stone with a tile infill.

Cool and durable, clay tile is a good choice for a full-sun porch overlooking a vineyard. Dusty red tiles are set off by stacked stone pillars that curve into arches supporting the timber-framed roof.

Concrete

Dyes and stains have changed the face of concrete; it's not your run-of-the-mill sidewalk material anymore. A poured concrete floor can give your porch a modern, one-of-a-kind look. And though concrete work is usually reserved for experienced professionals, it can be fun to experiment. One client spent a weekend stenciling a geometric pattern onto her existing concrete porch floor, painting it in subtle grays and tans. That was seven years ago and it still looks great. The key to her success was using high-grade paint, specially formulated for concrete.

A crisp line of white posts does more than simply hold up a porch roof. When square (but not unadorned) posts repeat at the same intervals as those standing between windows, the house seems to stretch toward the water.

Posts and Columns: Choosing the Right Support

Why posts *and* columns? Aren't they the same thing? Not really, though the terms are often used interchangeably. Technically, a post is any long piece of (square or cylindrical) wood or other material set upright into the ground to serve as a support. A column is a supporting pillar consisting of a base, a cylindrical shaft, and a capital. So you see, all columns are posts, but not all posts are columns. When architects talk about columns, they're usually thinking of something classical, whereas a post may suggest something as utilitarian as a no-frills metal tube set directly into concrete.

It's safe to say that all porches (by virtue of having roofs) need posts to hold them up. Some porches have columns (and railings) too, and when they do it's important they all work in concert. But first there are structural considerations:

How many posts do you need? Your engineer or architect should begin by calculating the minimum number—and maximum spacing—of posts required to handle the structural load of your porch roof. A rule of thumb: Posts that support the roof should be placed no more than 8 ft. to 11 ft. apart in order to keep the beam above to a manageable size. If you're adding a handrail, you may want to also add another supporting post between balusters. To ensure a safe and rigid handrail, we recommend a support every 5 ft. to 6 ft. You can engineer exceptions to these rules, but if you go wider you'll need more support from above, which will cost more.

There are rules that dictate how far apart to place posts and columns, and then there are exceptions to those rules. A post-and-beam porch allows you to keep view-blocking lumber to a minimum.

Twin porches balance the façade of a stately brick home. Highly embellished posts, detailed balustrades, and fanciful brackets and trim add to their perfect proportions.

Low to the ground and generously curved balusters create a mesmerizing rhythm. Rounded shapes are accentuated by a white-on-white color palette and substantial, squared posts.

Where should they go? Your posts will set up a rhythm that moves the eye across your elevation, so an overall composition must be established. Take note of windows and doors to prevent blocking views and circulation flow. Be careful to align posts with the foundation piers supporting the porch floor.

What size should they be? As always, proportions are critical; post height is directly related to how tall your porch ceiling will be and where the porch roof will hit the house itself. Tall columns should be proportionately wide; shorter columns less so. As a rule, substantial posts are more pleasing to look at than spindly ones.

Thoroughly Modern Millwork

Trim work and details are the features that can set a porch apart from its plain neighbors, but elaborate woodwork requires upkeep. These days, you can get a finely crafted look with none of the disadvantages of wood—if you're open to using new materials. Although it's true that synthetic materials can cost more —in some cases 50 percent more than wood— they require less maintenance and they last longer. These are a few of the materials we like:

• Cellular PVC is a wood substitute made by shaping polyvinyl chloride. It won't split, cup, rot, warp, or twist, and is perfect for trimming porch foundations and constructing porch skirts. You can work it like wood (using traditional wood-working tools), which means you can use it for fascias as well as brackets and custom molding.

• Composites (or blends of PVC or resins and wood) entered the market as decking, but they have made the transition to trim pieces and boards. These products are fairly consistent in terms of color and they can be routed and shaped much like wood. Some manufacturers seal the composite material with an acrylic shell, which provides even greater weather resistance and makes it easier to paint.

• Other composites made from marble dust, resin, and polyurethane, or Fiberglas-reinforced polymer products, are also available. These composite columns are load-bearing and architecturally correct. They can be cut to length, and come with a lifetime warrantee. The only complaint that we have ever had is that they can appear a bit "too perfect" for those who want an authentic period look.

• MDF (medium density fiberboard) is a material that can be worked like natural wood, but has a resistance to weather that real wood cannot offer. Exterior-grade MDF can be purchased in sheets, just like plywood, and used for everything from column brackets to raised panels on exterior porch walls. Because it won't expand or contract, it's a good choice for wrapping structural posts made of metal or pressure-treated wood.

It's hard to miss the attention-getting presence of a balustrade. Decorative balustrade panels are a defining feature of ornate and colorful Victorian-style structures.

Railings: Letting Form and Function Guide You

They're usually the first thing you see from a distance, and more than anything else, they define the style of a porch. Although posts play a strong supporting role, decorative handrails and balustrades are the stars that catch your eye and make an otherwise plain porch shine.

Railings are necessary features of most porches, but they also give homeowners an opportunity to express their style and personality. Before you begin, here are some basic considerations:

Decide if you need one. Local, state, and national building codes often require that a guard system be installed around the perimeter of a porch if it is more than 30 in. above grade. Whether open or closed, such a railing system must be at least 36 in. high. If you choose an open-rail design, bear in mind that the vertical pillars (or balusters) that run from the top rail to the bottom must be positioned close enough together so that a 4-in. sphere cannot pass between them. Many building codes also establish minimum and maximum dimensions for the handrail itself. We can't stress this enough: Check with your local building inspector to determine specific code requirements in your area.

Determine if the railing should be open or closed. Style and use will help you decide whether to go with a balustrade you can see through, or with a solid wall instead. If you're concerned about preserving your view, an open balustrade system is probably your best bet. If you have a contemporary home, you might even consider a post-and-wire or post-and-clear-glass system, both of which afford a nearly unobstructed view.

Railing Glossary

- **Handrail:** The bar at the top of a balustrade (or alongside stairs) that provides guidance and support and protects against falls.

- **Baluster:** One of a series of small pillars that fits under the handrail and extends either to a bottom rail, to a step, or to the floor.

- **Balustrade:** The combination of a handrail and a baluster, and the optional bottom rail.

- **Bottom rail:** An optional horizontal bar into which the ends of the balusters can be fitted.

- **Newel post:** A post at the top or bottom of a stairway; larger in scale than balusters and usually more detailed.

- **Post:** Any long piece of (square or cylindrical) wood or other material set upright into the ground or floor to serve as a support.

- **Column:** A supporting pillar consisting of a base, a cylindrical shaft, and a capital.

BALUSTRADE DETAIL

— Cap

— Handrail

— Post

— Baluster

— Porch floor

Give careful consideration to spacing between posts and rails. It's usually more visually appealing to evenly space posts and the balusters between them. Carpenters have a variety of formulas for determining spacing, some more convoluted than others. Basic math prevails. Once the number of posts and the distance between them is determined, you can figure out how many balusters you'll need, provided they comply with the 4-in. rule. Remember that handrails and posts will need to provide each other with surfaces where strong, secure connections can be made.

Style possibilities abound

After you've nailed down your basic parameters, you can have some fun designing a porch railing and the balusters that give it charm. There are essentially two ways to do it:

Be true. If your home is of an unmistakable style, you may want to be historically correct and/or interpret an architectural detail found elsewhere on your house, inside or out. If you're not exactly sure what a circa-1865

Railings are required if your porch stands more than 30 in. off the ground, but they don't have to be obtrusive. Horizontal wires extend from the house to supporting posts on a small, modern porch, preserving the view.

As long as a porch railing and balustrade are engineered for strength and safety, there's no limit to the amount of ornament you can add. Turned and fluted columns support an elaborately detailed porch frieze while relatively short balusters ground the porch from below.

125

Supported underneath for extra weight, a railing can be built low enough to do double duty as a bench.

Victorian porch should look like, there are reprints of antique stylebooks available to help. These are books that craftsmen used to develop styles for their local clientele, and they're a wonderful resource for architects and builders today.

Be creative. If your house has no specific architectural detailing or is more eclectic in style, you may prefer to take an entirely different tack by installing a balustrade that is unique to your home. Your choices are many: There are lathe-turned balusters available in a wide array of styles; clean-lined, square balusters; and flat, ornamental balusters made with scroll-saws, whose detailing is limited only by the imagination.

For a unique look on a cabin or lodge porch, you may want to consider making balusters from logs and/or branches. Just be sure they're treated with a clear wood preservative and used where they will be allowed to dry quickly. Remember: You can always add a railing even if it's not required by code—and that gives you a lot more design leeway.

Forget balusters altogether. A private porch in a wooded setting is adorned with wood panels into which a unique tree pattern is carved.

Posts, Plain and Fancy

Posts often announce a porch's personality so picking just the right style is essential.

A country porch is casual and relaxed, with gently embellished square wood posts.

Fluted columns and Corinthian-style capitals contribute to a formal look.

The rustic look of bare logs make for an artful entry.

Anything goes, as long as it is structurally sound and blends with the style of the house.

In the Arts and Crafts style, you'll often find posts set on substantial bases (or plinths).

Kneewalls and other options

On some house styles, including Craftsman, Shingle, and Victorian, you're likely to have a solid, partial wall around the perimeter of the porch rather than a balustrade system. This wall, also called a kneewall, can provide some protection from wind and rain, as well as a sense of enclosure.

A kneewall doesn't have to be solid; it can also be made of lattice panels set in wood frames. We like clear cedar lattice with lathes that are 1 in. thick for a substantial look and feel. Whether painted or left natural, these panels will last for a long time. Try experimenting with the negative space created by cutting into the lattice. The openings between lathes is only 1 in. square "window" spaces cut into the lattice. The opening can be framed to provide a "picture window". This window can frame a special view and lend interest to the porch, especially if it is a shape other than square.

Sometimes the best balustrade system is none at all. A low, solid wall, called a kneewall, provides a sense of shelter around the perimeter of a grade-level porch.

Kneewalls and screened porches can sometimes make it difficult to keep porch floors clean and dry. Small trapdoors placed intermittently along the bottom rail can be flipped open when necessary so that dirt, water, or blown snow can be swept through with ease.

Tempered glass panels are often used on more contemporary porches; they're especially effective when used to surround porches overlooking drop-dead views.

Wood Alternatives That Work

Although we like some contemporary materials, such as steel and tempered glass or steel and wire, we have to admit that in our practice we use wood components for our handrail systems almost exclusively (many of our projects have a traditional country-house flavor). That said, there are a number of versatile, low-maintenance wood alternatives available today. Here's how they compare:

	PROS	CONS	CONSIDERATIONS
WOOD (Cedar, redwood, cypress, north-eastern white pine, locust, pressure-treated wood)	• Can be worked with traditional woodworking tools • Many prefab wood components (handrails and balusters) are available at competitive prices • Many woods have a natural resistance to rot and decay	• Must be sealed with paint, stain, or clear finish to protect against weather, water, and UV rays • Vigilant maintenance is required to maintain good looks, condition, and longevity	• Regional availability (redwood is harder to obtain in the Northeast than it is in the Northwest) • Fast-growth materials may not have the same resistance to weathering as old-growth forest products • Wood prices are all over the place. They range from inexpensive for a pressure-treated wood rail system to very pricey for an ornate, custom-shaped system of old-growth cypress or redwood
SYNTHETICS (High-density urethane and molded polymers)	• Weatherproof • Very little maintenance required	• Molding process doesn't always allow for sharp detail • Usually sold as part of a system, so customization can be limited	• Expansion rates for some materials are high, so installation instructions should be closely followed • Initial cost can be higher than wood, but upkeep and maintenance costs are lower
COMBINATION MATERIALS (Vinyl wrapped around a pressure-treated wood core)	• Provides both strength and rot resistance • One of the least-expensive options • Virtually maintenance free	• Detailing isn't always sharp • Style choices are limited	

Nothing says "Come, let's sit and chat," like a porch with wonderfully ornate and colorful parts, whether they are made of wood or not.

A simple porch design welcomes the view.

Another more contemporary option is to create a kneewall of vertical tempered-glass panels, which will allow for an unencumbered view between the top and the bottom rails.

One thing to consider when using kneewall systems is how you'll get rain and snow off the porch floor. Some systems are designed with gaps between the bottom of the wall and the floor to allow for drainage. Others have routed openings at set intervals around the base. One of our favorite ways of handling the problem is to place little trapdoors intermittently along the bottom rail. These can be flipped open when necessary so that dirt, water, or blown snow can be swept through with ease.

Steps: Taking Them One at a Time

Any set of stairs will take you from level to another, but we like to think that porch steps are harbingers of comfort to come. A pleasant porch experience begins with the location of your stairs (where they provide access and how) and the way the steps themselves feel underfoot.

Remember that the stair, the porch, and the entry to the main house are all part of one composition. How your stairs open to the street or yard determines the ease and angle of a visitor's approach. Where you stand and what you see when you climb to the top are equally important.

Do you want the porch landing to align with a door? Or would you rather travel along a path on the porch before reaching the entrance to the house? Steps leading up to a simple covered entry should take you directly to the door with no detours, but a little meandering is OK enroute to a secondary, private porch.

Broad, deep steps are much more welcoming than those that are steep and shallow. We attribute the comfort level to something we call rise and run ratios. The "rise" refers to the riser, or the vertical part of a step, whereas the "run" refers to the tread, the horizontal part where your foot lands when climbing. To achieve a comfortable, easy climb, the riser should not be too steep or strenuous and the tread should provide plenty of room to plant your foot without crowding. If the riser is too high and the tread too shallow, you run the risk of turning an ascent into an aerobic exercise.

Local building codes have a lot to say about stairs; most require a tread to be at least 9 in. deep and a riser no more than 8¼ in. high. Obviously, there's room for some flexibility, so we recommend that you find a stair that feels comfortable to you and take a few measurements. The actual

Why settle for one set of stairs? A strong, accessible presence is established when visitors can reach a porch from more than one place. Balance, symmetry, and practicality all are enhanced if a site and budget will allow facing stairways that direct guests to a common meeting place at the top.

There's no question which way is in when plant-topped posts stand sentry for stairs that are wider at the bottom than they are at the top. Wide stone steps signal a greeting, and a decorative keyhole lattice sets a gracious tone.

A porch ceiling can be simple and plain, but where's the fun in that? A narrow porch that wraps a curve at grade is topped with a dynamic patterned ceiling whose tight, narrow slats create movement overhead.

number and size of your steps will depend on your house, site, and porch height, but it's a place to start.

What materials are best for steps? Here's where we like to think outside the box. A wood porch floor may make wood steps seem logical, but we sometimes prefer combinations: wood with stone or stone and brick.

Ceilings: Ideas You Can Use Overhead

The ceiling may not be visible to anyone standing at a distance, but it is a large part of any porch, and its features—height, color, texture, and degree of finish—establish a character for the space. Open framing and natural materials, for example, reinforce an outdoor attitude, whereas painted coffering or a gridwork of beams on a high flat ceiling create a more formal feel.

Ceiling materials

A traditional choice is beadboard, either painted or stained, which gives a porch a finished but casual look. Beadboard panels can be made of real wood or one of the newer, more durable composite materials. Tongue-and-groove cedar is another option. Cedar is available with a natural, rough texture or sanded for a more finished appearance. A more rustic choice is to leave the rafter structure exposed. In this case, you'll want your framing carpenters to know that their work will be on view so they take care to trim neatly when framing the porch roof. Because it will be visible, the choice of roof sheathing (the material above the rafters and under the shingles) is

A primitive porch calls for steps that match. A wide, comfortable stairway made of native stone is an ideal complement to a rough-hewn railing and posts.

The downside of some porches is the way they shut out light from above. An open gable in the roof solves this problem handily.

The grid formed by exposed rafters lends interest to the ceiling on an airy, secluded porch. A dropped overhang adds more angles, and with them visual variety.

important too; select one with a finished grade. Both rafters and sheathing can be painted or stained, depending on the overall look desired.

If there's one problematic thing about porches, it's the way they can darken interior spaces by blocking light from above. One way to address the problem is to incorporate skylights or an open gable into the ceiling roof. This allows natural light to penetrate to the back wall of the porch, brightening both the porch and the spaces next to it.

Clearances and sightlines

A high ceiling creates the open, airy feeling that is so integral to porch living. Although the minimum ceiling height for habitable space is 7 ft., 6 in. by code, we believe that the inside/outside nature of porches demands something taller. One way to achieve a higher ceiling height, at least over

Sanded cedar boards appear more formal and finished than rough cedar. The rich wood grain creates warmth and shadows, especially where the boards intersect on the porch corner.

A broad space surrounded by greenery enhances the outdoor experience. The ceiling, painted blue in keeping with classic porch tradition, suggests openness and sky.

The beadboard ceiling mirrors the color and pattern of the floor and kneewall contributing to the porch's simple country style.

portions of the porch, is to slope the underside of the roof instead of opting for a flat ceiling.

Remember that one's perception of ceiling height is also influenced by supporting beams, which typically run between porch posts, slightly below the ceiling proper. If they're too low, you may feel the need to crouch to get a better view, so we recommend 8-ft. ceilings, with beams placed out of your line of vision. If you plan to install ceiling fans, which can obstruct views, you may want to go even higher.

Porch ceilings have traditionally been painted light blue, the color of the sky. The belief, we've been told, was that it would fool wasps into sensing that it was the sky—and hence not a good place to build a nest. We can't promise it works, but we will attest to the fact that a soft blue ceiling can look lovely indeed.

Although the pitch of a roof can dictate a particular roofing material, sometimes anything goes; a sod roof is as natural as it gets.

Roofing: Creating Shelter from Above

When planning out your porch roof, protection should be your primary concern, but there are other things to consider: shape, slope, and materials, among them. You may be inclined to match the shape of your porch roof to that of your house, but it's not mandatory. On a smaller scale, a different shape may complement the house nicely.

The slope, or pitch, of your roof will often determine the best roofing material, as some are more suitable than others. Asphalt and cedar shingles are generally not recommended for shallow-sloped roofs. The minimum slope required by manufacturers of asphalt shingles (to warrantee their products) is 4-in-12, which refers to a roof with a slope that rises 4 in. for every 12 in.

The greater the slope, the more options you have. Here's how to decide which slope is best for your porch roof, and what roofing material to use:

Ridged metal provides contrast when placed next to traditional clapboard siding on a house with a shingle roof.

Flat roof

No roof should be constructed to be absolutely flat. That said, we often design porch roofs that are essentially flat, allowing a deck or a second-story porch to be built above. A flat roof also allows you to maximize the interior height of the first-floor porch while still fitting the porch under second-story windows. Flat roofs are often embellished with balustrades around the upper perimeter for a decorative touch. The best material:

EPDM (Ethylene Propylene Diene Monomer). We prefer this rubber roofing membrane because of its durability, design versatility, and relative ease of installation.

Common Roof Shapes

- **Hip**, which rises in inclined planes on all sides. The line where the two adjacent slopes meet is called the hip.

- **Gable**, which slopes up from only two walls. A gable is the triangular portion of the end of the building extending from the eaves to the ridge.

- **Shed**, which has only one slope, with only one set of rafters extending from a higher wall to a lower wall. It's also called a lean-to roof.

Shallow slope

Any roof that's nearly flat to one with a pitch of less than 4-in-12 is considered to have a shallow slope. The best materials:

EPDM. An excellent low-slope material.

Metal. Copper is a beautiful, long-lasting choice, but it can be expensive. An alternate metal is galvanized steel or metal roofing with a baked-on, paintlike finish. Coated metal is versatile, durable, and colorful. When using metal roofs in climates with snow, we suggest you install "snow dogs," small, upright fixtures that prevent large sections of snow from sliding down the roof onto plantings or people.

Steep slope

A roof with a slope of 4-in-12 or more is considered steep. Because these roofs are able to easily shed water and snow, you can choose from a wider variety of roofing materials. The best materials:

Asphalt shingles. An economical and long-lived roofing option, 40-year architectural shingles are tried and true (architectural shingles have more texture and depth than common builder shingles).

Cedar shingles. Cedar roofing includes both cedar shingles and cedar shakes. Shingles are more refined, with a consistent texture and thickness, whereas shakes are more rustic and have a hand-worked look. Western red cedar is the most common choice for cedar roofing, but you may prefer Alaskan white cedar, which ages to a silver-grey.

Shadows play on the walls and floor of a lakeside porch because the roof is sheathed in Plexiglas panels. Natural light bathes the side of the house, where windows transfer the sunshine indoors.

It takes only a few details to make a porch stand out, along with the house it's attached to: A small gable signals the main entrance and scrollwork brackets and a low, turned balustrade provide charm.

Slate. Original to many old houses, natural slate is famously long-lived. It's readily available but can be expensive. Because slate is substantially heavier than most materials, your porch structure must be designed and engineered to bear this extra load. Note: Many synthetic slate products are available, including some made from concrete tiles, ceramics, and recycled rubber, but their longevity has yet to be determined.

Concrete and clay tiles. Like slate, these are heavy and long-lasting. They're typically used in more temperate climates, because they are easily damaged by freeze/thaw cycles.

Plexiglas and glass panels. A great way to maximize natural light, these transparent/translucent roofing materials provide weather protection, too.

Brackets, Molding, and More

The basic structure of a porch could not be simpler: It's a roof covering a platform. But few of us are satisfied with that bare-bones approach to architecture, and we find it irresistible to add layers of detail to make something simple that much more interesting and personal.

Although some architectural elements have functional roots, many have evolved for decorative purposes only. Gussied up or not, a porch shouldn't show up the house to which it is attached. A word to the wise: A porch festooned with architectural details and trim can overwhelm an austere façade. If you have your heart set on a dressed-up porch, we suggest you get some extra trim and give the rest of the house a dose of the same detailing.

Redirecting Water

Even roofs that we call "flat" have a slight slope designed to shed water, so some thought should be given to how that water will be directed. A small gable can be useful in redirecting water flow away from porch steps, or you can use gutters. Choose from applied gutters, usually of copper or aluminum, or integral gutters, which are framed as part of the roof and not usually visible from below. The jury is out as to whether gutters are an overall help or hindrance in regions where snow, leaves, and ice are issues, but they do control water runoff quite effectively.

Sweetly curved profiles and delicate scrollwork adorn column brackets, which are frequently used to dress up an otherwise plain design.

A typical porch provides many opportunities for adding embellishment. Here are a few:

Eave brackets. Soffit or eave brackets originally helped hold up roof overhangs. Now nearly always decorative, they can reinforce the overall architectural style of the house, from simple to ornate. For maximum visual impact, we recommend that you don't skimp on the size.

Column brackets. When required structurally, these brackets connect supporting columns to the roof, extending up and across the roof beam and ending under the soffit. We now include these brackets—often adorned with open work and curving profiles—primarily for their good looks.

Fascia molding. This is the band that visually connects the porch roof to the house, often including a crown molding or a buildup of layers to produce shadow lines and visual interest. This is also the area where gutters will usually be installed. In classical architecture, this area is part of what is called the "architrave."

Frieze decoration. This area under the cornice and at the top of the wall is a perfect place for adding moldings and applied shapes.

Barge boards. This finishing touch to the gable is often coordinated with the fascia trim. It allows trim details to be carried up and across the gable slope.

Porch valance. Although this porch addition can function as a sun shade, it's mostly just for fun. It is a good place to make a design statement.

They're not usually structural anymore; today eave brackets are mostly for show. When there's enough textural contrast between brackets and walls, they can add a jolt of color and surprise.

(left) Applied trim is commonly used as frieze decoration, directly under the cornice.

(right) Carved wood "bunting" is an example of a porch valance, an ornamental porch addition which is lovely, but has no practical purpose.

149

Screened-in, safe, and comfortable, a bright and airy porch can be furnished to feel just like another room in the house—complete with lighting and overhead fan.

Bringing Power to Your Porch

One of the things we love best about porches is how they allow us to be outdoors while still enjoying the comforts of home, including light, heat, cool air—even running water. It's so easy to run electricity to a porch that we can't imagine why anyone wouldn't do it. Wire a ceiling fan and enjoy classic, cool breezes all summer long (see p. 182). Plug in a space heater for winter warmth. Add plenty of exterior-rated outlets and bring music, lighting, TV, movies —even your laptop—into the mix. Utilities are certainly not required, but they do make a good porch better.

Adding electricity

Review your porch plan to assess your electrical needs. Consider how you want to light the space and how many outlets that will require. Our advice is to add more than you think you need, as your usage may change over time. The cost differential between one outlet or three is quite small, and it's certainly less than adding more outlets down the road. There may be limitations to the number of outlets your electrical service panel can handle, so be sure to call in a licensed professional. If you think you may want to enclose and heat your porch for year-round use in the future, keep in mind that no space along a wall can be more than 6 ft. from an electrical outlet.

Ceiling fans do their best work when dropped down no more than 10 ft. from the floor. Combined with natural breezes (even if they are few and far between), an overhead fan can keep the air moving comfortably on a hot summer day.

No matter how primitive or simple, a porch should be illuminated at night. A hurricane lamp housed in a metal lantern is hung high and out of harm's way.

Lighting the way

Overhead porch lights are practical and can add ambience, whereas chandeliers can highlight a dining table and small spots can illuminate a porch swing or glider. The best lighting plans include all three basic types of lighting: ambient, task, and spot. Ambient lighting includes all general lighting (the most common are ceiling fixtures) that is even and consistent over a large area. Task lighting offers a lot of flexibility; it can be placed next to chairs and on tables to facilitate reading, dining, or playing cards and board games. Spotlights are used to target a particular area or to bring attention to a doorway or an architectural detail.

Because ambient light reflects off walls and porches have few of them, it may be difficult to calculate just how much light you need. At minimum you should have a 60 watt incandescent bulb (or equivalent) on either side of an entry door about $5\frac{1}{2}$ ft. above the floor. In addition, we recommend that fixtures be placed at intervals of 10 ft. to 12 ft.; these can be flush-mounted ceiling fixtures, short-stem hanging fixtures, or, if your ceiling is enclosed, recessed fixtures.

You may not think you need to use fixtures rated for outdoor use, but we specify them anyway. Most fixtures are sold with a UL® (Underwriters Laboratories) rating, which means their electrical components have been tested and meet minimum safety standards.

Not all manufacturers can afford to submit products for testing, but that doesn't necessarily mean they are deficient. If you like a fixture that isn't UL rated, first ask your electrician to check your building code and insurance policy requirements, and then inspect the fixture to verify that it is up to UL standards.

Suspended from short-stem chains, copper lanterns provide practical overhead lighting while adding texture, detail, and ambience.

A built-in gas grill positioned near the door to the kitchen simplifies outdoor cooking and alfresco dining. An overhead vent prevents flare-ups and smoky situations.

Running water lines

Hot and cold running water is a nice feature that allows you to install a refreshment bar (practically a necessity on an entertaining porch) or a smaller utilitarian sink, which is great for quick cleanups. If a wet bar seems a little much for your porch, we recommend at least a simple hose bib to allow you to water plants and hose down the porch floor.

Bringing water to your porch (hot, cold, or both) is a straightforward process. Your only concern (in many climates) will be keeping your pipes from freezing in winter. If you install a drain-out valve you'll be able to easily drain the system each season. If you're installing a sink you'll need to provide for sink drains and a waste-water hookup. Because your porch is attached to the main house, an experienced plumber can make the necessary connections and route waste water easily to the plumbing system in the house.

Adding gas and grills

You may also want to consider having gas service piped in to fuel a fireplace, grill, or flickering gas lamps. If you already have access to a gas line, you can run it into the porch during construction with relative ease. If gas is a new power source for you, you'll have to choose between propane or natural gas, depending on what is available and most cost-effective. Some neighborhoods have gas pipes in the street, but in other areas you'll need to purchase bottled gas. Depending on the gas used, some fixtures will need to be fitted appropriately to ensure a good burning pattern. It is a good idea to have isolation valves installed, so if your fireplace or lamps ever need repair you won't have to shut down your entire gas line to do it.

If you like the idea of a gas fireplace, we recommend direct-vent units that can also provide a bit of extra warmth to make spring and fall porch

The clean lines of this porch make it a perfect companion to a modern cabin. "See-through" cable railings further maintain the view.

sitting more comfortable. Finally, keep in mind that although moody gas lamps look lovely on a porch, they won't do the job of electric lights. They're not designed for efficiency, but rather to imbue your porch with old-fashioned ambience.

Many older homes have what we'd call bare-bones porches attached. These are structures that serve mostly as transition spaces, not outdoor living rooms, and they're perfectly delightful—even without wet bars or atmospheric lighting. But as we design more and more porches for our clients, we find they enjoy a few more amenities like the ones we've touched on here. We'll go into greater detail in the next chapter.

A "Lantern" Lights the Way

The original façade of the house wasn't altered by the addition of the porch, which sits to the right and rear of the property and doesn't intrude on the streetscape.

This house already had a lovely neighborly porch out

Huntington,
West Virginia

front, but the homeowners, a retired couple fond of entertaining, wanted to host large-scale gatherings. They enjoy elaborate catered affairs, so they needed to improve on the quality—and volume—of their outdoor space to better suit their lifestyle.

The circa-1930s house was grand to start with, overlooking a large park in an established neighborhood in Huntington, the second-largest city in West Virginia. The spacious house is situated on a corner lot, but the homeowners' expansion plan required more room, so they purchased the property next door and tore down the existing structure. This gave them the space they needed to realize plans for their dream porch.

Bringing in the Light

The new porch is quite substantial, running the length of two sides of the house, with plenty of room for gathering. Its visual focus is what they call

The "lantern" is the center of attention, as well as the spot where both wings of the porch intersect. At night, it serves as a welcoming beacon for guests.

Sheltered under the "lantern" and out of the way of traffic moving from one wing of the porch to another, the dining area is defined as separate and special. The extra ceiling height adds drama.

the "lantern," a two-story corner section of the porch with a vaulted ceiling and clerestory windows around its top perimeter. This expansive space provides increased seating out of the general circulation area of the porch and its windows bring in abundant light to the back walls. Overhead fans cool the space in style. Stairs down from this area allow for easy transitions from the porch to the yard below.

Because the porch was designed for large-scale entertaining, the couple had to plan for deliveries of food and party supplies, such as tables and chairs. The design provided for a *porte-cochere*—a covered drop-off area—where trucks and caterers could pull up to load and unload in a sheltered spot. To keep the covered area from looking like a driveway, they set square stone blocks into the grass in an alternating pattern.

Pairs of columns establish a rhythm across the porch, while the mature landscaping that surrounds it provides shelter and cool shade during the summer months.

Striking geometric iron railings are anchored onto wide stone caps that ground the masonry stairs.

Porch materials were chosen to blend, but not exactly match, those used on the house and existing front porch. The brick, floor tiles, and stone caps of the new porch are quite close to the originals, but the woodwork, a new element, was designed to complement the existing house in style and scale.

The substantial fascia and frieze of the main house were reinterpreted on the new porch, allowing the two parts to look as though they were constructed at the same time. The wood posts on the new porch are a departure from the solid masonry on the existing porch; it's a change in materials that tones down the large scale of the addition, making it feel a little lighter and more open.

This big, beautiful porch works well largely because the homeowners were able to annex the land next door; without it, the site would have felt crowded by such a generously proportioned addition.

One of three stairways off the back porch, this one leads to another terrace. Broad treads and gentle risers encourage meandering on the steps and off the porch.

Porch detailing references the house, but is not slavish to it. Viewed from the backyard, the "lantern," fascia, and posts are clearly substantial, but the mix of materials keeps the addition in proportion to the main house.

An Urban Transformation

Most homeowners who live in a neighborhood that

Minneapolis, Minnesota

has seen tough times would relish the idea of an enclosed porch. For one thing, it captures more interior space, which is important when your home sits on a small lot in an urban setting. For another, it effectively shuts off the house from the street and the neighborhood beyond.

Christiana Kippels and Wayne Thompson are not most homeowners. When they moved into a small home with close-in neighbors on a tree-lined Minneapolis street, the couple chose to open up the enclosed porch and they gave their home a welcoming new façade in the process.

The couple felt the existing porch blocked light and views and isolated them from the music of the street. They felt good about their neighborhood and wanted to animate a part of it by revitalizing their home. It was fine to feel sheltered in winter, but they wanted to spend time outdoors in the warmer months. An outdoor "parlor" would encourage mingling, as well as monitoring of the street.

162

Inside out, this neighborly porch offers the best of both worlds: A comfortable outdoor living room and an up-close vantage point from which to survey the street.

It was important to ease the transition between public space and private property. The easy curve of the walkway makes the approach to the house comfortable and welcoming.

The door casing and house numbers highlight the Craftsman style.

A Creative Solution

A neighborly porch was definitely in order. Located under the main roof of the house, the porch design is eclectic, acknowledges Eric Odor of SALA Architects. "The heavy dormer and brooding brow of the roof were begging for something more substantial," he says, "but historically accurate options were not very appealing to my clients or me. So I got creative."

The styling has overtones of the Craftsman aesthetic, with deep overhangs, substantial posts sitting on a stone kneewall, and decorative brackets. The shallow arch that frames the entrance was drawn from Western parks buildings, says Odor, whereas the simply detailed wood posts are

(left) Large, detailed windows draw daylight into the house. Shingle siding and simple but distinctive casings around the windows add visual interest. Beadboard ceilings are punctuated with black fixtures and a gently arched opening frames the view.

(right) The porch is eclectic, but there are stylistic features that come together to create a cohesive, Craftsman-like look. Iconic bungalow-style posts are softened by recessed panels and slight tapering at the top.

more Craftsman in feel. The distinctive door and window casings were inspired by Greene and Greene's Arts and Crafts–style Gamble House in Pasadena.

A sedate color palette calls attention to architectural details and textures, including a stained beadboard ceiling, a wood floor, and shingle siding. Exposed rafters and the integrated roof tie together the different parts of the home in both a visual and a practical way. The homeowners now enjoy a home with more character, and an inviting, open porch that welcomes neighbors instead of shutting them out.

A Clean, Green, Treetop Retreat

What do you do with a big box of a house built in the

McLean,
Virginia

1970s, back when stark and dark were the bywords of contemporary architecture? Ronda Cole was faced with that dilemma when she moved into a 3,500-sq.-ft. home in McLean, Va., a suburb of Washington, D.C.

For all its space and surrounding trees, the house had no personality and no connection to the outdoors. Cole wanted light and "windows all around," and she wanted to keep construction green, so tearing the place down and starting over was not an option. She wanted privacy and comfort, and she wanted to enjoy her lovely wooded lot in any weather.

She called in architect Lorena Checa, who describes her design as "instinctive and completely informed by the land." The result was a home reborn as treetop retreat, complete with a gazebo-like screened porch that sits away from the house but is connected by a suspended bridge.

Looming over trees and a walkway to the front of the house, the modern screened porch is linked to the main house by a connecting bridge with views on both sides. Surrounded by nature, the porch creates a feeling of separateness and solitude.

The porch beckons all the way from the other end of the house, where trees flank a walkway and frame a view of the distant space that seems to be floating in air.

Going with the flow of the home, the connecting bridge leads into the kitchen; beyond it, only a few more steps bring visitors to an open deck.

Stepping Lightly on the Land

The modern, fan-shaped porch looms over wooded walkways, its roof sloping from 8 ft. to 12 ft. high at the widest part of the structure. Broad screen panels open up the views. "We wanted the space to be sculptural and to feel as though it was about to take flight," says Checa.

Standing two stories tall, this porch isn't for the faint of heart. Built on round steel pillars the color of tree trunks (six under the porch and two adjacent to the house), the porch "steps lightly on the land," says Checa.

The homeowner can access the porch from her breakfast nook off the kitchen. She can see it from anywhere in the backyard and from below on the side path that directs guests to the rear.

The porch shape echoes the half-circle foyer in front. Its curves soften the steep, wild lot, as well as the sharp and angular house to which it is attached. It connects visually to the surrounding decks, which are wrapped with durable steel cable rails that seem transparent. Checa chose a warm gray paint that weathers well and redwood accents on railings for contrast and warmth. Deep overhangs protect the porch from rain, snow, and the hot summer sun.

With an eye on green design, Checa used environmentally friendly materials throughout the renovation, including Trex, a composite material made of plastic and reclaimed wood, on the porch and surrounding walkways and decks. To keep intrusive lighting to a minimum, the architect used outdoor lighting judiciously and added dimmers inside.

The success of this project, she says, is how comfortable it *feels* on the property, and how well it stands in harmony with nature.

There's a sculptural balance between the free-form porch and the severely angular contemporary home that was reborn, thanks in large part to the addition of the new porch.

Curves soften the edginess of the fan-shaped space. The porch has a light industrial feel with steel bolts and wires; its roof rafters stretch across the ceiling, open-armed, to the sky.

CHAPTER 4

The Finishing Touches

Once your porch nears completion, you'll want to start thinking about how to make it feel like home. Because almost all porches are casual places, they lend themselves to furnishings that are not too fussy, often pieces that are crafted locally and have a personality. There are literally hundreds of choices in outdoor furniture, but we recommend that you put comfort above all else. Think flea-market finds and fabrics that can take the wear and tear of an outdoor space. Unless you're furnishing an elegant entertaining porch, we suggest you don't try to match everything perfectly; there's something honest and warm about a porch that has been furnished with a variety of styles, colors, and textures.

As you were designing your space, you probably had an inkling where you wanted your furniture to go. Now is the time to fine tune that general plan. Remember that what works in theory may not translate exactly in

Porch adornments tend to be casual, in keeping with the nature of most outdoor rooms. Twig chairs with accent pillows and a few potted plants are all it takes to provide a warm welcome.

practice. Plan your furniture arrangement by selecting major pieces (chairs, lounges, tables) and placing them so that they facilitate traffic flow and take full advantage of the views or focal points that are part of the space.

Furniture That Fits

Just as you would consider design and function when furnishing a room in your house, you need to do the same when choosing your furniture and fabrics for outside. Even if your porch is mostly protected, assume that whatever you place on it will be subject to the sun and/or rain on occasion. Keep in mind that some materials are more resilient than others, so read labels carefully, ask questions, and check out manufacturers' websites to find out if the material you like will hold up over time.

Here are a few choices to get you started:

• Wicker is probably the most iconic type of porch furniture; whether simple or embellished, it has been popular for more than a century. Wicker can be left natural, stained with an accent color, or painted (traditional porch colors are white or dark green). Wicker should not be exposed to the elements for any length of time, so position it toward the back of a porch in a sheltered spot whenever possible and remove it for storage during cold weather. Wicker fibers should be kept slightly moist because they will crack if they become too brittle. Unpainted, unvarnished wicker should be misted now and then to keep it from drying out completely.

• Synthetic wicker is usually made from polyester resins and aluminum framing, and unlike the real thing, it can be exposed to the elements without damage. It comes in a natural wicker tone or traditional white and green, so you can get the look without the upkeep.

Durable porch and patio furniture can be dressed up or down. A quartet of comfortable wicker chairs is complemented by classical garden pieces, including statuary, sconces, and topiary planters.

There's no better place to mix and match than on the porch. A natural Bar Harbor–style wicker set looks all the more airy and curvaceous against the backdrop of stark white Adirondack chairs.

- Wood, painted or stained, is another traditional choice; think Adirondack chairs and picnic tables. Your choices are many; longtime favorites include teak, cedar, redwood, and cypress, but on a protected porch even pine or maple can be used as long as the finish is maintained. Woods such as pine, fir, and oak should be treated regularly with a quality paint, stain, or wood sealer.

- Twig or willow furniture has a carefree, rustic look. It's often produced locally, and can be found at farmer's markets, craft stores, or even roadside stands in the country. To prevent shrinking and loosening of joints, it shouldn't be exposed to direct sunlight. Keep it sheltered in a covered area to prolong its life.

- Wrought iron or cast iron is a very heavy and durable material that looks great on formal porches. It's less likely to break than wicker or wood, but at the same time, its weight can be a detriment. It's difficult to move, prone to rust, and requires regular maintenance.

- Aluminum furniture is rustproof, lightweight, and usually more expensive than wrought iron furniture. Most aluminum pieces come with a baked-on enamel finish. Look for a thick, heavy-gauge material and smooth, welded seams and joints. Quality varies, as does cost.

- Plastic is inexpensive, lightweight, and readily available, but it comes in a limited number of colors and styles. Resin chairs are great for extra seating, and because they are often designed to stack they can be stored easily. What plastic lacks in good looks it makes up in ease of maintenance. Plastic porch furniture needs only to be hosed down occasionally to keep it clean.

Wood seating offers the best of both worlds: weather-proof durability and the classic look of Mission furniture. Circling a round patio table, curved slat-back benches fill a tight spot with plenty of room for guests.

A porch can provide a new home for castoff furniture. An eclectic mix of whitewashed wood chairs is repurposed with style when surrounding a gracious table prepared for a formal dinner.

A quick online search or visit to any patio furniture outlet will reveal an extraordinary range of furniture choices available: You can select anything from dining tables and chairs to end tables, benches, swings, ottomans, and chaises. If you're planning to host dinner parties, you'll want a large table that seats at least eight, or perhaps several smaller tables that afford more flexibility. If your porch is small, a bistro table for two is perfect for a secluded corner of your space. No matter your table size, you can create a gracious alfresco dining atmosphere by using linens, dinnerware, and centerpieces, just as you would indoors.

Adding Fabrics

Fabrics lend a feeling of warmth to a porch, and nearly every kind of furniture we've mentioned can be fitted with removable cushions for comfort. The colors and patterns you choose can help define your decorating style. For occasional use (pillows or runners or anything that will come inside at the end of the day) you can choose almost any fabric that appeals to you. If you expect that your porch fabrics will spend the entire summer outdoors, you should go with durable, water- and stain-resistant materials instead. Look for fabrics that breathe, are mildew resistant, and don't fade too easily. Sunbrella® and other tough, solution-dyed acrylics are specifically made to endure the rigors of weather, harsh sunlight, and lots of use. Natural fabrics such as canvas, duck, and twill are traditional choices that look great, but because they don't resist mildew well, cushion covers should be constructed so they can be removed for washing. Laminated cotton with a polyurethane or acrylic coating will resist moisture, but it should be used only in sheltered areas to prevent fading.

Flea-market finds (or Grandma's old kitchen set) are at home on the porch. Cool colors refresh old wood, which should be properly sanded first, then sealed to protect against the elements.

The Enduring Rocking Chair

No one knows exactly who put the first rocker on a chair, but Americans like to take credit for it. Some say it was Benjamin Franklin. Others say the rocker originated in England in the early 1700s and made its way to the colonies around 1740, where it was immediately embraced.

Early rockers were made by simply notching the legs of a chair and attaching them to curved slats. Over time, rocking chair design evolved, and there are literally hundreds of interpretations available today—much to the delight of porch sitters everywhere.

What make the porch and the rocker such a perfect pair? In the 18th century, outdoor furniture was mostly made of wrought iron. Wood, though much more comfortable, didn't stand up to the elements quite as well. As the porch grew in popularity, with its sheltering nature and proximity to the main house, so did the idea of bringing comfortable chairs outside. With its tall back, deep seat, and charming style, the gently moving rocker was a natural. Porches and rockers have been inseparable ever since.

Some rocking chairs are better known than others, thanks to the famous people who sat in them. Mark Twain was photographed sitting in a plantation porch rocker, President Lincoln had a favorite (upholstered and definitely for indoor use), and in the 1960s John F. Kennedy gave the rocker a little glamour when he insisted on bringing one into the Oval Office. A favorite photo of the flamboyant Pablo Picasso shows him sitting in a classic Thonet® rocking chair.

Not every rocking chair is designed to last over long periods of time on an open porch. Some woods can handle weather better than others; they include teak, painted mahogany, fir, and cedar. Although wicker and rattan chairs look great, they should be used only on the most protected porches and never left out for long periods of time. You can also find rockers made of synthetic materials that look for all the world like wicker and rattan but don't require anywhere near the same upkeep and care.

Many fabrics wear well on the porch furniture, thanks to advances in textile technology. Canvas and other natural fabrics look great, but most should not be left outside indefinitely.

Shade Solutions

Add atmosphere to your porch space with shades, blinds, and curtains, which can also block the sun as needed and provide privacy and seclusion. They're also a great way to add color. For a more natural look, choose split bamboo or wood matchstick blinds. Canvas awnings are another popular option. These can be simple panels you pull up and down or broad coverings on metal frames mounted to the exterior of the porch. Awnings can be extended or retracted as the sun moves around your property. If you decide to use curtains or blinds outside, be sure that all your hardware is made of brass, bronze, or stainless steel to better resist rust.

A well-furnished outdoor room is a delight until the sun shines in. Roll-up shades can prevent fabrics from fading and keep a space feeling comfortable when the glare of harsh sunlight heats things up.

Floor Show

Whether you choose wood, brick, or concrete flooring, consider adding an indoor feel to your porch by laying down a rug. The right rug can define sitting and dining areas and make a space feel "finished." Naturally moisture-resistant rugs made of sisal and hemp are available in neutral colors with great textures. Sisal can even be painted with fabric dye or latex paints for a unique look. A floor cloth made from primed canvas is another way to add personality; seal it with several coats of polyurethane to protect your design and clean it easily with mild soap and water. More traditional rag rugs or cotton patterned rugs are good choices, too. Be sure to place a pad underneath to grip your rug and prevent slipping.

Fan Fare

With a little attention to detail, ceiling fans, a decidedly functional feature, can make a decorative statement on your porch. With so many styles available today, you can choose the perfect fan to reinforce the mood you've already established on your porch with architecture and furnishings. Your choices range from tropical fans with wide rattan paddles for sprawling verandas to simple stainless-steel fans suitable for contemporary porches.

Just search "ceiling fans" online and you'll be blown away by the options. Before you decide, though, consider your unique situation and the features you'd like your ceiling fan to have:

• How high should you go? If your porch has a typical 8-ft. ceiling, you can manage with a minimal-clearance fan that sits close to the ceiling. If it has a cathedral ceiling, your fan will need an extended shaft to bring the fan blades closer to where breezes can be appreciated. We like to place fans 8 ft. to 10 ft. above the floor for the most efficient cooling effect. The minimum height of any fan, including attached lights, should be 7 ft. If you are mounting your fan on a sloped ceiling, be sure the motor mount will accommodate this angled installation.

• Want light? You'll definitely want to have two switches installed: one for the light and one for the fan so that they can be used independently. A dimmer on the light is another nice feature to include during installation.

• Need a remote? Many of today's fans are equipped with three or more speeds to suit the seasons, and many come with remote control devices so there's no need to keep getting up to adjust speeds with a wall switch or pull chain.

• Ask directions. Most fans can move air in two directions: up and down. A fan pulling air upward makes a space feel cooler, whereas a downward-moving fan can move a warmer, upper layer of air down to take the edge off a cool night.

• Play it safe. Porch fans should always have a UL listing for damp or wet locations to protect mechanical and electrical components.

• Protect your paddles. Be aware that some materials will weather better than others; a woven wood paddle will not last as long as a plastic or stainless-steel one. Wood can warp, whereas veneers may be more stable. Choose according to the level of exposure your fan will get on your porch.

• Size it right. Paddle size is determined by the size of your space. If a fan is too big, it may look awkward and out of place. If it's too small, it won't do its job properly. Most manufacturers will indicate the maximum area for a fan's efficient use. A rule of thumb: A 15-ft. by 15-ft. space requires a blade span of 50 in. to 56 in.

Touches of Greenery

Because they are an outdoor extension of your home, porches are enhanced when you incorporate plants, flowers, and the surrounding landscape into their overall design. You can do this by adding window boxes, trellises, hanging baskets, and pots for hardy plants.

Take nature a step further by planting flower beds on both sides of the walkway leading up to the porch, then placing similar plants on your porch steps in a variety of containers.

Fragrant plants are ideal because you enjoy them up close on a porch. And plants that are said to repel insects, such as citronella scented geranium, can be both attractive and functional.

When planning plants for your porch, consider style, architecture, and scale. If you have a formal, traditional house and porch, choose symmetrical plantings with restrained shapes. If, on the other hand, you live in a simple farmhouse, you might do better with the unstructured, abundant look of a cottage garden.

There are two caveats to consider when outfitting your porch with greenery: First, water is damaging. Drainage from pots, window boxes, and hanging baskets should be controlled with pot saucers or be allowed to drain away from the porch out into the landscape (see p. 108). Second, growing conditions vary for all plants—even those safely planted in pots. If a flowering plant requires full sun and your porch is mostly shady, it will never flourish. Any well-stocked nursery has options for all kinds of conditions, so ask questions before you buy. A good source for independent advice is your local cooperative extension.

Well-tended plants in hanging baskets grow full and flower, adding color to a country porch. Because there are so many varieties available, the foliage can be chosen to coordinate or contrast with other porch adornments.

Flowering plants look even better growing in unexpected containers. Tins, teapots, and (lined) twig baskets are just a few of the decorative choices to consider.

Planting in Pots

Containers are perfect for porches; even the smallest space has room enough for a lush corner of colorful flowers or a modest kitchen garden complete with herbs you can snip on the spot to spice up summertime meals.

Container gardening has increased so much in popularity that you can now find pots and planters in all sizes and styles at stores ranging from Target® to Home Depot®—and everywhere in between. Garden centers and online catalogs offer some unique and decorative choices. Just about any container can be modified to function as a plant container, from old wheelbarrows to wooden tool boxes, but there are a few things to consider:

• Material matters. Cheap plastic pots usually deteriorate when exposed to strong sun over time. Terra cotta pots allow evaporation through their walls and can dry out very quickly. Glazed pots last and look good, but they need adequate drainage holes in the bottom to allow extra water to drain out of the soil.

• Be wary of wood. Wood containers such as window boxes, half barrels, tubs, and custom-made planters are popular, but they are susceptible to rot. Redwood and cedar resist it better than most woods, but beware of woods treated with preservatives such as creosote or other toxic compounds that can damage plants. We wouldn't recommend using them for plants you plan to eat.

• Regular watering is required. Containers exposed to full sun and wind may need to be watered daily, which can be a chore. There are, however, small drip watering systems that can handle this task for you. These systems are most efficient when a number of pots are grouped in one area and the drip lines are run from one pot to another.

- Soil should be plentiful. It is usually a good idea to use containers that have a soil capacity of between 15 and 120 quarts. Their mass will prevent plants from drying out too quickly.

- Raise containers up. It's important to keep containers and their saucers off the porch floor and up on legs or even brick, to allow for drainage and airflow under the pots. This, in turn, will protect your porch floor and/or railings from mold and water damage.

Hanging a Swing or Hammock

Swings and hammocks are a wonderful addition to nearly any porch. You can easily hang a swing from a beam on the roof of your porch, but keep in mind that not all ceiling ratters are substantial enough to hold the extra load of a swing and its occupants (check with your engineer or contractor before you start drilling holes). If you know in advance that you'll want a swing, you can double up a rafter during construction. If not, a swing frame can be constructed of wood or metal and attached to a porch beam. We strongly suggest that a long eyebolt be predrilled through the beam or rafter and secured with a large flat washer and locking nut. Under no circumstances should you use eye screws installed vertically in the ceiling joists to hang a swing, because this type of connection will eventually work its way loose. Use 2 chains to hang the swing seat:

When positioning your swing, be sure to allow enough clearance for the full arc of the swing, so you won't hit a wall, rail, or other furniture.

A hammock is usually attached to porch posts or to a post and the house wall, but you can avoid drilling by opting for a hammock frame instead. They allow flexibility, and because hammocks take up so much floor space, you can remove them conveniently as the need arises.

A neutral color palette comes alive with greenery in clay pots. By varying the height, weight, and texture of plants, areas of interest are created on a narrow porch.

Vines and Trellises

With or without trellises, vines are a wonderful way to add color, provide privacy, and cool the interior of your porch. Their random growth pattern blurs the boundaries between porch and garden. They grow quickly and spread widely, which is a good feature—unless the growth gets out of hand. With a little foresight, you can control vines, keep maintenance to a minimum, and let them do what they do best: hide unsightly views and cool south-facing porches in the hot summer months.

There are three kinds of vines: twining, tendril, and clinging vines. Twining and tendril vines climb best on wires, trellises, and arbors, whereas clinging vines climb independently, using disklike adhesive tips or aerial rootlets along their stems. Clinging vines can be used on brick or masonry but not the walls of wood-frame buildings. They cling so closely to walls that moisture can collect under them and cause rot. In fact, we hesitate to use them even on masonry walls because they can compromise mortar joints, although the damage is evident only over time.

Vine supports should be constructed with sturdy materials. This is especially important with substantial vines such as wisteria, which has been known to pull down entire walls. Copper and aluminum are preferred because they resist rust. Wood structures can be made of rot-resistant woods such as redwood, cedar, or cypress, as well as the less attractive but more durable pressure-treated woods.

Vines and other climbers worth trying

There are vines suitable for most growing areas—and most porches. Some grow fuller than others; some fairly burst with color whereas others remain lush and green. Here are a few to consider:

Wisteria is a fast-growing vine that does well when supported by a sturdy trellis or other strong structure.

Planted alongside a small entry porch at the side of a house, climbers can be trained to gracefully curve around an arched opening and frame the doorway beyond.

Perennials

These grow slowly the first year, but rest assured they are busy establishing a root system that will sustain often prodigious growth the next couple of years.

• American Bittersweet. This is a twining vine that grows 10 ft. to 30 ft. a year. It has orange and yellow fruits, does not die back in winter, and requires sun to part shade for best growth.

• Trumpet Vine. This clinging vine grows about 15 ft. a year and may die back, depending on its location. It produces large red-orange flowers and requires full sun.

• Virginia Creeper. This is a clinging vine that uses tendrils with suction cups for climbing. It grows about 10 ft. a year and does not die back. Although it's not a flowering vine, it turns deep red in fall and produces a very dense screen.

• Wisteria. Wisteria adds fragrance and a touch of elegance to any porch, but it requires a sturdy means of support. Some varieties can grow about 8 ft. a year, and they may die back in winter.

Annuals

Plant seeds of these vines at the base of a trellis or post as soon as the soil is warmed by the spring sun. If you space the plants fairly close together you will most likely have a dense screen by early to mid summer.

• Hyacinth Bean. This twining vine covered with purple flowers and pods can reach a height of 15 ft. in a single summer.

• Black-Eyed Susan. Growing to about 6 ft., this twining vine is graced with yellow and orange flowers with chocolate brown centers.

• Cathedral Bells. This twining vine grows to 15 ft. and has rose flowers.

Black-Eyed Susan vine.

Though some grow slowly in the first year, climbing vines will rapidly gain strength and wrap themselves around porch columns, softening the look of so much wood against the landscape.

Climbing roses

Another traditional plant that looks wonderful clambering over porch posts and rails is the climbing rose. It has no tendrils, so it will need to be tied to a trellis or other structure. Check with your local cooperative extension office to verify your growing zone before choosing a rose, because many are not hardy beyond zones 4 or 5.

The following are hardy to zone 3:

• 'William Baffin' rose has pink flowers in June, with a slight rebloom in July and good rebloom in August and September.

• 'Henry Kelsey' is a red rose that has good June bloom and a slight rebloom in July, but then rebounds with blooms in August and September.

• 'John Davis' is a pink rose with great fragrance. It blooms nearly nonstop.

The nice thing about porch adornments is they are not forever. Colors and styles will change over time, as will your taste in fabrics and furnishings. Flowers will come and go; shrubs and vines will continue to grow over the years. You can add decorative seasonal touches, or subtract them as you desire.

If you live in your house long enough, you'll see life play out on the porch. The entertaining porch where you host weekend dinner parties now may be the site of a full-fledged family reunion one day. The privacy porch where you take your morning coffee may become the quiet place where you go to rock a baby to sleep.

Change is good; it's what makes your porch a dynamic place, a stage with great possibilities. If you get the bones right, anything goes. The important thing is that your porch complements your home and enhances your lifestyle.

There's no question in our minds: Life is just better out on the porch.

Climbing roses are delicate and don't flourish everywhere, but clustered around the railing of a gazebo-like porch they're a stunning summer adornment.

The House of
Many Porches

Although this home had sweeping views of the Catskill

**Dutchess County,
New York**

Mountains, Jimmy knew it could still stand some improvement: It was
the perfect candidate for a porch or two. Doug and Sarah, the new homeowners, wanted to renovate much of the interior of the farmhouse-style
colonial, improve the views, and add a substantial master suite, complete
with an outdoor shower.

Jimmy saw a great opportunity and added an elegant, rounded porch
that could be accessed from the master bedroom through two sets of
French doors. A towering stone fireplace stands sentry between them.

Despite its size, the porch feels private and cozy. It helps connect the
house to the landscape and to the pool area that sits a short distance away.

Stately wooden columns create a rhythm, establishing boundaries for
this porch—which is really more like an outdoor room—whereas a conical
roof gives it definition from a distance. Indigenous stones were used for the
chimney and the low stone walls that encircle the space. The curved ceiling

Under a great domed ceiling on a porch with a powerful presence, a towering fireplace crafted of native stone steals the show.

rises with the rafters, so a great deal of the imposing stone chimney is visible. When sitting out on this porch with a fire blazing, it feels like you're camping on the edge of a rock outcropping, looking down into the valley below.

When In Doubt, Add More Porches

About four years after the project was completed, the homeowners decided they wanted the rest of the original house to match the level of detail introduced in the addition. Jimmy proposed some major changes.

The house already had a wraparound porch, but it was plain at best and the homeowners felt its proportions were off (they were right). In its place, Jimmy designed a sweeping, two-level porch with rounded corners for gathering.

On the main floor, the handrails on the wide front steps are splayed in welcome. From there, the front door opens to the foyer and beyond to the dining room and living room. At the side, there are doors to the kitchen and mudroom. Over the porch, Jimmy designed an open deck that can be accessed by two separate bedroom suites on the second floor.

The new porches improve the view, but more than that, they give the home a presence it didn't have before.

Wide balustrades lend formality and balance to the front of the house, whereas in the back the shapely porch adds intrigue and interest. Both create an important transition from large house to sprawling property and help to extend the seasons for the homeowners. At garden parties at this home, people flow seamlessly inside and out, onto the porches, and beyond.

With room to create a rhythm, the rounded edges of a two-story porch do wonders to seamlessly ease the large home into its landscape.

High above the property and overlooking the valley below, the second-story deck is as much a privacy porch as it is the perfect vantage point from which to take in an extraordinary view.

Stairs are sometimes thought of as secondary, but they're worth a few carefully designed details, such as splayed handrails and turned newel posts.

An elegant outdoor space requires furniture to match. A closely woven wicker suite is striking in black with bold striped cushions.

A Victorian Gem Emerges

It took quite a leap of faith on the part of innkeepers

**Hot Springs,
North Carolina**

Karen and Peter Nagle to revive this home in the small town of Hot Springs, N.C. The house sits in a broad, lush valley, where it had been an integral part of the community's history. But the old place had been so badly remodeled by its previous owners that its Victorian roots were barely discernible.

Among other unfortunate "improvements," the entire upper floor had been removed and an ornate porch stripped from the front of the house, rendering it little more than an architectural curiosity.

The single-story house had strange proportions at best, yet it appeared as though a Victorian gem lay entombed underneath its aluminum siding. The homeowners were intrigued by an unexpected richness of detail throughout the home.

The Nagles had access to historic photographs that provided clues that they were dealing with what had once been a grand home. After much

The home's Victorian charms were rediscovered, even as the home-owners took some liberties with the original design. The new porch was extended across the house to balance its position on the landscape and to provide more outdoor living room.

Stunning surroundings can now be viewed comfortably from the porch that was recreated on the Mountain Magnolia Inn. The house sits in a lush, green, North Carolina valley, which more than did its part to inspire the project.

Dining tables are often set for formal dinners, with linen tablecloths, fine china, and flowers.

Rich woodwork and interior details continue out onto the porch. Painted posts and an arched valance call attention to the valley view beyond.

investigation and research, they drafted a plan with Architect Jane G. Mathews of Asheville, N.C., to resurrect the home. The interior work was painstakingly accomplished over time. Later, the elaborate front porch was recreated, providing an attractive front entry, views of the valley, and an ideal dining spot for guests of the Nagles, who had newly reopened the house as a bed-and-breakfast, the Mountain Magnolia Inn.

The detailing for the porch came directly from the original photos; the railing, post, and valance are close interpretations of what originally existed. Not surprisingly, a few liberties were taken with the overall design. The porch and the upper porch rail were extended across the whole front of the house, whereas the original ended at the square tower.

Wide French doors leading from the formal rooms on the first floor out to the porch allow the two spaces to complement one another. The interior and exterior now have a sensible connection, and because the climate is relatively mild in North Carolina, the porch is in full use for three seasons.

The homeowners were delighted to restore beauty and drama to a home that had gone from a fanciful grand dame to an ill-proportioned, aluminum-clad shadow of its former self. The romance is back: The Magnolia is rich with ornament once again, and with a charming porch emblematic of its rediscovered high Victorian style.

Details were kept consistent. At left, the baluster rail links the porch to the bay window and the balcony above. Broad stone steps lead from the terrace up to the porch and straight on toward the front door. Striking trim colors were chosen to make the woodwork detailing stand out.

The porch is open and airy, with a hint of Victorian formality. When the tall French doors are thrown open to the entry hall, guests can move seamlessly inside and out. Chairs and tables can easily be spaced apart for solitude or clustered together for socializing.

ARCHITECTS